Contents

Acknowledgements

I would like to acknowledge the help given by numerous individuals with the research on which this publication is based. Wendy O'Conghaile and Robert Anderson, Senior Research Managers at the European Foundation for the Improvement of Living and Working Conditions, Dublin, responsible for the transnational research project of which this research formed a part, have made many valuable comments on drafts of this report. My colleague John Benington has made a major contribution to the ideas which have informed the research programme. The following people provided invaluable access to local partners for the interviews used in the three case studies: Carola Bell (Western Isles and Skye and Lochalsh LEADER project coordinator); Bob Lawrence (North Tyneside City Challenge) and Elaine Snaith (North Tyneside Metropolitan Borough Council); and Trevor Cornfoot (Coventry and Warwickshire Partnerships) and Kevin Hubery (Coventry City Council). I am particularly grateful to all those involved in the three local partnerships who readily agreed to be interviewed and whose views are reflected in the research, and to Joyce Liddle who undertook the interviews for the North Tyneside case study.

PARTNERSHIP AGAINST POVERTY AND EXCLUSION?

Local regeneration strategies and excluded communities in the UK

Michael Geddes

First published in Great Britain in 1997 by

The Policy Press
University of Bristol
Rodney Lodge
Grange Road
Bristol BS8 4EA

Telephone: (0117) 973 8797
Fax: (0117) 973 7308
E-mail: tpp@bris.ac.uk
Website: http://www.bris.ac.uk/Publications/TPP

First published as Working Paper No WP/96/29/EN, *The Role of Partnerships in Promoting Social Cohesion – Research Report for the United Kingdom*, by the European Foundation for the Improvement of Living and Working Conditions (1996)

Cover photograph: traditional cooperative methods of tweed making reflected in a Gaelic language course in Ness on the Isle of Lewis, in the area covered by the Western Isles and Skye and Lochalsh LEADER I partnership.

ISBN 1 86134 071 0

Michael Geddes is Principal Research Fellow and Research Manager at the Local Government Centre, Warwick Business School, University of Warwick.

The Policy Press works to counter discrimination on grounds of gender, race, disability, age and sexuality.

Cover design by Qube Design Associates, Bristol.
Printed in Great Britain by Antony Rowe Ltd, Chippenham.

List of figures and tables

Figures

Table

Part One: National overview

Introduction

The research for this book was undertaken in 1995 and early 1996 as part of a transnational research programme conducted by the European Foundation for the Improvement of Living and Working Conditions on 'The role of partnerships in promoting social cohesion'. When reviewing its work on issues of social cohesion during the past decade, the Foundation recognised the growing importance of a partnership approach, while noting that it raised a number of policy and research issues (Ball, 1994). The research programme aimed to assess the contribution of the partnership approach to combating problems of poverty and social exclusion, and to suggest guidelines for policy makers for the future. These issues have been given added relevance in the UK by the decision of the recently elected Labour government to set up a new Cabinet unit to coordinate policies to tackle social exclusion.

In many European Union (EU) and member state programmes aimed at building social cohesion and combating poverty, unemployment and exclusion, establishing local partnerships has gained increasing importance in recent years. The aim of such arrangements is to harness the energy, skills and resources of the key players who develop and implement local regeneration strategies. These include public sector agencies, employers, trade unions, voluntary organisations and local community groups. These partnerships take different forms and their work covers a range of social, economic and environmental policies. They often focus on a specific local area such as deprived urban neighbourhoods, underdeveloped rural regions, or neglected housing estates.

However, while the principle of local partnership is now quite widely accepted, there remain too few examples of partnerships which can demonstrate lasting impact in tackling poverty and social exclusion on a broad and multidimensional basis. Little evidence is available about the relative advantages and disadvantages of different models and structures of partnership, and about the outcomes for different partners and stakeholders, including those directly involved and those with a wider interest in the success of local initiatives. While there have been a number of evaluations of specific programmes and partnerships at

European, national and local levels, there has been little cross-national and cross-programme assessment. In this context, the objectives of the transnational research programme were to:

- document and assess the extent to which the local partnership approach is being adopted within EU member states in programmes concerned with promoting social cohesion;

- document and analyse the perceptions of public, private, voluntary and community partners on the success of such partnerships and the problems encountered;

- develop guidelines and recommendations to assist policy makers and other interested parties in developing future partnerships aimed at tackling social exclusion.

Preliminary research (Geddes, 1995) for the programme identified a number of questions and research issues concerning the representation of interests and organisations in local partnerships; the strengths and weaknesses of different partnership structures and working practices; the scope of their activities; the resources available; and the evaluation of their impact on poverty and exclusion. It also suggested that such local partnerships tend to exhibit a number of key characteristics. The research was therefore focused on local partnerships which:

- are based on a formal organisational framework for policy making and involve implementation on the ground in disadvantaged areas;

- mobilise a coalition of interests and the commitment of a range of partners around a common agenda and multidimensional action programme;

- aim to promote local development and regeneration and combat poverty and social exclusion.

Within the transnational research programme, research studies were undertaken in 10 member states of the EU, including the present research study for the UK (the other nine, available from the European Foundation, are for Austria, Belgium, Finland, France, Germany, Greece, Ireland, Portugal and Spain). Each national research study included a number of elements, and these provide the structure for this publication:

- an overview of the national policy context for local partnership, including the nature and extent of problems of poverty and social exclusion, and with special reference to the policies and perspectives of different partners and interests (Chapter 1);

- a 'portfolio' of examples of local partnerships, illustrating different dimensions of current practice (Chapter 2);
- in-depth analysis of the structures, working methods and outcomes of local partnerships by means of three detailed case studies (Chapters 3 to 5);
- conclusions and policy recommendations for those involved in partnerships at the local level and also for national and EU programmes (Chapter 6).

The final stage of the research involves preparing a European synthesis report drawing on the findings of the national research studies.

Chapter 1

Local partnerships and social exclusion in the UK

Introduction

In recent years partnership has become one of the fundamental principles in policy making and implementation not only in the UK but more widely in the advanced industrial countries (OECD, 1995). In the UK the emergence of a local partnership approach to problems of poverty and social exclusion is associated with several linked factors: the perception of partnership as a perceived solution to a range of complex policy problems; the increasing role in public policy of business, market models and managerial methods; an emphasis on localised responsibility for policy implementation; and the growth of poverty and social exclusion.

Partnership and public policy in the UK

 Partnership has become one of the vogue words of the 1990s in the UK policy community. The principle has been applied to a range of policy sectors – from education and training, to housing, community care and social services, and community and urban regeneration. Government, business, local government, community organisations and voluntary sectors increasingly subscribe to the value and virtues of partnership.

The partnership approach has a considerable history in the UK, but it has been implemented in different ways in different periods. During the 1970s, partnership was a central plank of government urban strategy with the creation of Inner City Partnerships in major cities. However, those partnerships were designed primarily to coordinate public sector responses to urban decline and to integrate the efforts of national and local government departments. The community sector was involved only at the margin and the private sector was a relatively minor player.

Since then, during the 1980s and 1990s, successive governments in the UK have instituted a far reaching restructuring of the public sector. Although the objectives were the 'rolling back of the state' and the reduction of public expenditure, the outcomes have also been to create fragmentation and organisational proliferation within the public sector, including the creation of many new state and quasi-state agencies, including local-level agencies. As a result, in many areas of public policy there is a much greater need for partnership within the public sector itself. The 1980s also saw a general shift to 'market' as opposed to public sector-led policy initiatives. Government encouraged a more 'business-like' state, with a stronger role for the private sector in setting and implementing the policy agenda (Jessop, 1994). In relation to urban policy, this was reflected in the view that:

- lasting economic, social and environmental regeneration requires the active involvement of the private sector;

- making urban areas attractive to the business community will bring wider benefits including 'trickle-down' effects such as job creation;

- the role of elected local government should be reduced in favour of agencies involving business leaders and government officials (Harding and Garside, 1994).

In this period, partnership predominantly involved the public sector providing mechanisms and incentives which would encourage the private sector to take the lead in local regeneration. The emphasis of the previous partnership model was reversed to one of private–public partnership, with the private sector presumed to play the leading role.

The policies of the 1990s have to some degree recognised the limitations of that approach, and have introduced a more inclusive conception of partnership. In the sphere of urban regeneration, the focus has shifted from a narrow preoccupation with physical regeneration to a wider concern with the economic and social regeneration of communities. Social as well as physical investment has become an important element in partnership programmes, and this has brought with it the involvement of 'community' interests alongside the public and private sectors.

Important programmes in this respect are City Challenge, New Life for Urban Scotland, and the Single Regeneration Budget (SRB) Challenge Fund, the successor to City Challenge. Competition between localities remains the preferred method of allocating scarce resources. However, these programmes have wider remits than their predecessors and offer a more important role to local government, local communities and the voluntary sector. The SRB has particularly emphasised strong local partnership as the basis for a successful bid for funding. Regional Challenge and Rural Challenge schemes also adopt a partnership format.

The current model of partnership as the framework for regeneration at the local level reflects the union of several factors:

- the perceived intractability and complexity of urban problems, requiring a multi-agency approach to both economic growth and competitiveness and disadvantage and deprivation;

- the development of a 'mixed market' in the delivery of many services, requiring collaboration between public, private and voluntary sector providers;

- the proliferation of state and quasi-state agencies;

- the development by many local authorities of 'enabling' or 'civic leadership' roles which emphasise a partnership approach;

- pressure from grass roots and local community organisations, sometimes as a consequence of the fact that traditional forms of local democracy do not necessarily allow local communities adequate involvement in the policy process;

- the recognition that while private sector involvement may be essential for local regeneration, market mechanisms alone are unlikely to be effective, and the private sector may only wish to take on a limited responsibility for local regeneration and particularly for social issues (Darke, 1995).

Partnership and local governance

A feature of the growth of the partnership approach in the UK is that strong central direction of policy by government has been combined with policy delivery through partnership mechanisms at the local level. The implementation of national policy programmes through local partnerships has been dubbed a 'new localism' in public policy, combining elements of urban managerialism, competition for resources, and the involvement of a variety of local interests in a distinctive manner (Stewart, 1994). Partnership has become a central feature of a new model of local governance, both creating and reflecting changing relationships between the three spheres of the state, the 'market' and civil society.

Poverty and social exclusion in the UK

While some of the facts and issues remain strongly contested, there is much evidence showing that the UK has been experiencing a widening of social inequality and a serious growth of poverty and deprivation.

There has been a larger recent growth of poverty in the UK than in any other EU member state, and a faster rate of growth of inequality than in any other industrialised country with the exception of New Zealand (Gaffikin and Morrissey, 1994a; 1994b). Some commentators see more in common between the experiences of the UK and US than between those of the UK and most other European countries, pointing to the way in which similar economic policies in the 1980s were associated with a polarisation of the labour market.

There are different measures of poverty in use in the UK, but they all show a growth in poverty and inequality during the 1980s and 1990s. Between 1979 and the end of the 1980s, the numbers of those living on or below 50% of average income grew from 9% to 22% of the population. The share of national income of the poorest 20% of the population fell from 10% in 1979 to 6% at the beginning of the 1990s (Oppenheim, 1993). During this period, this group appears to have failed to benefit from economic growth, something it had managed to achieve during the rest of the postwar period (Joseph Rowntree Foundation, 1995).

The growth in inequality in the UK can be attributed to a number of factors:

- more people are dependent on benefits, both as a result of higher unemployment and demographic factors;

- the income gap between those with earnings and those dependent on benefits has widened;

- differences in income from work has grown rapidly.

By the early 1990s there were more individuals and households below the poverty line in the UK than in any other EU member state (Eurostat, 1997). The growing gap between rich and poor is seen to be damaging the social fabric and weakening social cohesion, with a substantial minority of the population having no stake in the prosperity of the country. A recent report by a Commission of Inquiry into Income and Wealth – established by the Joseph Rowntree Foundation and with members from a range of stakeholders including major industrial and financial interests, the trade unions and the voluntary sector – con-cluded that the economic costs of poverty are substantial. Increasing inequality can also be damaging to economic competitiveness, if the latter depends on systematic investment in human and physical capital (Joseph Rowntree Foundation, 1995).

Certain social groups are more at risk of poverty than others. Members of ethnic minorities are nearly twice as likely as other social groups to suffer poverty because of unemployment, because of differentials in education and qualifications, but also because of discrimination (Amin and Oppenheim, 1992). Recent figures show that more than 60% of adults receiving income support are women, as are 65% of those on wages below the Council of Europe's decency threshold (Oppenheim, 1993). Social change is increasing the numbers of single parent, largely female, households who are particularly at risk of poverty and are likely to have very limited capital as well as low incomes.

The growth of poverty and inequality has also produced intensified geographical disparities between prosperous and deprived areas. The concentration of intense poverty has increased in recent years, especially in large urban and old industrial areas. There is a marked concentration of minority ethnic groups in these 'extreme poverty' areas, including both inner-city areas and peripheral housing estates (Green, 1994). In some areas of most concentrated deprivation, poverty threatens to overwhelm the investment made in people and the physical fabric. There is also growing awareness of the scale of rural poverty (McLaughlin, 1994).

Increasing recognition of the widespread and structural nature of poverty and social and economic polarisation has in turn been associated with the notion of social exclusion. The term social exclusion is intended to recognise not only the material deprivation of the poor, but also their inability to fully exercise their social and political rights as citizens. Further, it suggests that where the material living standards and citizen rights of significant numbers of people are restricted by persistent, multiple and concentrated deprivation, social cohesion is threatened. As the concept of social exclusion has become more widely accepted, there have been important shifts in perspective from previous understandings of poverty:

- from a focus on income and expenditure to a wider view of multidimensional disadvantage;

- from a static picture of states of deprivation to a more dynamic analysis of processes;

- from a focus on the individual or household to a recognition that it is also within communities that disadvantage and exclusion are experienced (Room, 1995).

Social exclusion is a contested concept. It can be argued that it implies a potentially inclusive and cohesive society which is at odds with the realities of class and other divisions, and that it posits an oversimplistic polarisation between the 'included' and the 'excluded' (Levitas, 1996). However, exclusion can also be seen as a potent 'alliance' concept which opens up possibilities of building bridges between those disadvantaged to different degrees and by a wide variety of social, economic and political processes. It need not imply any less concern with the essential economics of poverty, and with distributional policies, but may help to link these to related questions of social and political participation and power.

In this context, partnership at the local level may be seen to reflect the need for spatially targeted, multidimensional and multi-agency strategies for excluded communities, including the involvement of excluded groups themselves, alongside mainline social and economic programmes. But the development of a partnership approach to problems of poverty and social exclusion in the UK is also part of a much more general trend to institute a partnership approach to public policy. This is being impelled by the redefinition of the respective roles of the public and private sectors, the reshaping of state agencies, and a search for innovative solutions to pressing problems of both economic growth and competitiveness and social cohesion in a context of resource constraint.

Local partnerships in the UK

Current policy context

Successive national governments in the UK have promoted a general philosophy of partnership and shaped the arena for local partnerships. The partnership approach appears to be endorsed, albeit with significant differences of emphasis, by all the main national political parties.

During the 1990s, the Conservative government increasingly required local projects funded by national programmes to demonstrate a framework of local partnership. The main recent UK urban regeneration programmes such as City Challenge, New Life For Urban Scotland, English Partnerships and the SRB were implemented through local partnerships. City Challenge was launched in 1991 with the aim of providing greater coherence in urban regeneration policy. Resources for up to five years were allocated to local partnerships of local authorities, the private sector and local communities, on the basis of competing bids presented to the Department of the Environment, Transport and the Regions.

In 1993, a further radical shake-up of urban policy, involving the merging of 20 previously separate programmes administered by five different government departments, led to the introduction of the SRB. SRB funds are allocated by competitive bidding and negotiation with government Regional Offices, involving bids from local partnerships comprising public, private and voluntary sector organisations, usually, but not necessarily, led by local authorities and/or Training and Enterprise Councils (TECs). Bids are expected to meet some of the following objectives:

- enhance local employment, education and skills, especially among disadvantaged groups;

- lever in further resources, from the private sector and European funding;

- encourage economic development and local economic competitiveness;

- improve the environment and housing, including tackling crime;

- enhance health and quality of life;

- increase community participation.

Bids are also expected to be good value for money and show a comprehensive and targeted approach.

A total of 201 successful bids were announced at the end of the first annual bidding round, out of 469 applications. These were projected to lever in four times the SRB investment, create 300,000 jobs and generate 20,000 businesses, as well as achieve other social and community advantages (Mawson et al, 1995).

Some of the ideas embodied in City Challenge and the SRB have since been applied in rural areas through the Rural Challenge scheme. Started in 1994, Rural Challenge offers resources to local partnerships in rural development areas through a competitive bidding process.

In Scotland, the Scottish Office (a department of UK government) has been not only a partner in the New Life for Urban Scotland partnerships, such as Castlemilk, but the lead partner. In England, in contrast, government is not usually a partner in local regeneration projects, although it is a key stakeholder. In this context, the role of central government is in setting the framework of policy and funding for local partnerships through successive programmes; allocating resources between competitive locally generated bids, including specifying the bidding criteria; providing guidance to local partnership projects and monitoring and evaluating their performance. Government currently emphasises the benefits of the competitive model of resource allocation, which has been a feature of recent funding programmes, in ensuring that funding goes to the best local projects, including those able to demonstrate the commitment of a range of partners. Government officials argue that the UK model of local partnership has a number of successful features, reflecting political commitment at national level. These include:

- local partnerships involving all the key players, linked to but separate from the local structure of government, with their own budgets, and strong management;

- time-limited action plans, with key outputs and milestones to implement an overall strategy;

- projects which demonstrate benefits to local people and can demonstrate success;

- effective performance monitoring to reward success and penalise failure.

However, even when national government is not itself a partner in local partnerships, an increasingly important role is being played by national agencies such as English Partnerships, the agency charged with reclaiming vacant and derelict land. While English Partnerships is able to act as developer in its own right, most of its powers are designed for working in partnerships and in addition to its mainstream resources it has a Community Investment Fund for locally generated non-profit-making projects (English Partnerships, 1995). Although government is not directly involved in local partnerships, integrated Regional Offices have been established to decentralise the administration of urban policy, along with a new Ministerial Committee for Regeneration. These changes represented a measure of response by the recent Conservative government to criticisms that policy coordination is inadequate and the outcomes of urban policy fragmented and limited (Robson, 1994).

Policy statements from the other main parties in the UK also indicate strong support for partnership. The Liberal Democrats have sponsored a Commission on Wealth Creation and Social Cohesion, which agues in its report (Dahrendorf, 1995) for a stakeholder economy and a social framework of inclusion. Similar ideas have been promoted by the Labour Party. Labour in opposition has also strongly supported local public–private partnerships, emphasising the role played by Labour-controlled local authorities, and the party has maintained this stance since taking office. While there remain important differences between the positions of the main parties and the roles they would envisage in partnerships for different partners, there is nonetheless a broad political consensus about a partnership approach in the UK.

European Union programmes are increasingly important in supporting local partnerships in the UK. The recent Poverty 3 programme was of particular relevance because of its focus on poverty and social exclusion. However, the limited scale and relatively restricted funding of Poverty 3, compared with nationally funded programmes, has limited its impact in the UK context (Erskine and Breitenbach, 1994). The same is broadly true of the LEDA programme (Bennett and Krebs, 1994) which promoted local economic development initiatives. The LEADER rural development programme has had a more significant impact in rural areas in the peripheral regions of England, Wales and Scotland (Black and Conway, 1995), although rural issues are less prominent in a national context in the UK compared to some other EU countries.

Current forms of partnership

A local partnership approach to tackling problems of geographically concentrated deprivation and poverty has become a significant feature of current policy in the UK. A variety of models of local partnership can be identified.

Under the influence of recent government programmes, especially City Challenge and the SRB Challenge Fund, *formal multi-partner* local partnerships are active in many localities, especially in the larger urban areas. These *urban regeneration local partnerships* are frequently tackling problems of poverty and exclusion within a multidimensional policy framework which may include physical regeneration, business support, employment and local labour market interventions, environmental improvement and crime prevention and community safety. These partnerships are likely to be formally constituted as trusts or limited companies. The partnership structure will typically include a management board on which a wide range of partner interests are represented, a tighter executive committee of core partners, and a full-time partnership team. Partners are likely to include representatives from local government and other local public and quasi-public agencies, employers and employer organisations, voluntary organisations and the community. These partnerships are responsible for large budgets, and often for major 'flagship' redevelopment projects in town centres and on industrial and housing estates as well as training programmes, community facilities and a range of smaller projects. Examples of this form of partnership, described in Chapter 2, are the Castlemilk Partnership, Glasgow; North Tyneside City Challenge Partnership, and Coventry and Warwickshire Partnerships.

The current SRB is promoting the extension of this model to smaller urban areas and rural areas, although these areas still tend to lose out to larger urban areas. In general, the partnership approach appears to have developed more slowly in *rural areas,* although recently, as noted above, EU programmes, particularly LEADER, have stimulated a local multi-partner partnership approach. A feature of the partnership approach in many rural areas, reflecting the nature of the local economy, has been an emphasis on small enterprise and entrepreneurship as a solution to rural deprivation. Examples of rural partnerships discussed in Chapter 2 are the Western Isles and Skye and Lochalsh LEADER Partnership, and South Pembrokeshire Partnership for Action with Rural Communities.

A contrast to the broad urban regeneration policy remit of local partnerships, associated with recent government funding programmes, is provided by the local partnerships supported by the EU Poverty 3 programme, 1989-94. These initiatives also established formal multi-partner local partnership structures (although there tended to be fewer employer representatives and a greater number of community representatives) and developed multidimensional strategies and action programmes. However, the Poverty 3 local partnerships focused their strategies and activities much more directly on problems of deprivation, poverty and exclusion, and regarded the facilitation of processes of community development and empowerment as central to their agenda. Examples of Poverty 3 *anti-poverty partnerships* discussed in Chapter 2 are the Brownlow Community Trust and the Granby-Toxteth Community Project.

Local Poverty 3 partnerships also offer leading examples of partnership strategies and action plans focused on the needs and perspectives of specific *social groups*. The Brownlow partnership identified three key 'target' groups: women, children and young people, and the unemployed. The Granby-Toxteth partnership focused on the needs of the black and ethnic minority communities in the area.

The spread of the practice of local partnership, and the increasing tendency for funding programmes to require a strong partnership framework as a condition of access to resources, has led to a widespread development of *less formalised local partnership* arrangements. These may often initially involve lead activity by one agency (the local authority for example) but acting in partnership with other agencies and stakeholders. An example of this trend is the Rotherham Community and Economic Regeneration Strategy. In many cases these less formalised partnerships will have limited resources beyond those of the partner agencies themselves. However (as in Rotherham), many of these partnerships are actively seeking funding, and if successful this is likely to contribute to the formalisation of the structure and agenda of the partnership. The situation is therefore quite dynamic.

A development noted by some commentators (Peck and Tickell, 1994) is the emergence in some localities of '*nested tiers of partnership*' at different geographical scales. A local partnership within a deprived neighbourhood may coexist with a regeneration partnership for the wider urban area concerned, which in turn may relate to partnerships at the regional level. In North Tyneside, the City Challenge Partnership, discussed in Chapter 3, has been able to draw on wider partnership relationships between some stakeholders (particularly public agencies and business interests) at regional level. In many cases the relationships between partnership arrangements at different levels may be purely informal, but the Coventry and Warwickshire Partnerships illustrates a proactive attempt to develop a two-tier partnership structure.

Perspectives of partners

The wide application and diffusion of the partnership approach in the UK, both as a means of generating and implementing new solutions to policy problems and, frequently, as a condition for accessing funding, means that many partners, partner organisations, and agencies have developed well-formulated perspectives concerning their interests and roles in partnerships. There is extensive debate about the advantages and disadvantages of partnership and the contributions of different partners. The following section outlines the views and perspectives of the main categories of partners in local partnerships in the UK.

Local government

In many instances, local authorities are dominant or leading players in local partnerships concerned with poverty and social exclusion. More recent government and EU programmes have enabled local government to play an important role. At the same time local authorities have adapted to a partnership approach in many areas of activity having ceased to be monopoly providers of many local services. Among the local partnerships described in Chapter 2, the North Tyneside City Challenge Partnership and Coventry and Warwickshire Partnerships illustrate the leading role which local government can play.

In their service provision local authorities in the UK have become used to a framework of partnership. Many authorities have sought to develop a wider role of local community or civic leadership in partnership with other agencies and community interests. The proliferation of partnership schemes has led to growing recognition of its potential advantages as well as its challenges to the role of local authorities.

During the past decade local authority opposition to partnership with business has given way to a more pragmatic approach:

> Local authorities should work closely and in partnership with the private sector, at both a strategic level and in relation to particular initiatives. It is essential however that the private sector recognises that partnership is a two-way process. A positive commitment is required to the area or programme concerned. (ACC/ADC/AMA, 1994)

However, a wide spectrum of attitudes still remains. In some places where there is congruence between local authority and business interests, political and ideological views have changed significantly. Elsewhere, what may superficially appear as shared values and value changes may only be pragmatic accommodation (Darke, 1995). On the other hand, partnerships between local government and voluntary agencies to deliver services has traditionally been close and collaborative.

Local authorities see their role in economic and social regeneration partnerships as being rooted in the electoral legitimacy of local government, and its responsibility to represent the interests of the whole of local society, not merely sectional interests:

> The social and economic challenges facing local communities today require local government which can both provide community leadership and enable communities to govern themselves. [Local authorities] extend choice to those who cannot compete in the marketplace. They enable those who can participate to do so and safeguard the interests of those who cannot. They offer community leadership ... working in partnership with all parts of their communities, including the private sector and voluntary and community organisations. (ACC/ADC/AMA, 1995)

The extent to which local authorities can realise this role depends on the success with which they can make a variety of contributions to local partnerships (Roberts et al, 1995). Such contributions can include financial, physical and human resources, the use of local government powers and the delivery of services.

However, working in partnerships makes heavy demands on the human resources and management and other skills of local government officers and elected councillors. The resources which local authorities can commit to partnerships are constrained by a severe and long-term squeeze by central government on local expenditure. Many authorities recognise that local government itself could often do more to target resources to deprived areas (ACC/ADC/AMA, 1994), but they also look for a more equal partnership with central government as the context in which they can fulfil their own potential in local partnerships:

> ... it is now time to rebuild consensus and re-establish the idea of partnership at the core of the relationship between central and local power. (ACC/ADC/AMA, 1995)

In recent years a significant number of local authorities have attempted to develop more strategic and corporate local anti-poverty strategies in partnership with other agencies and local communities. The national associations of local government have established an Anti-Poverty Unit to advise local authorities on poverty issues and the development of anti-poverty strategies. A National Local Government Forum Against Poverty has been set up to campaign politically on poverty issues.

Other state and quasi-state agencies

As is the case with local government, there is also wide recognition by many other local agencies of the desirability of a partnership approach. Agencies such as health and hospital authorities and TECs frequently play an important role in local partnerships. A public–private partnership framework at a local level is particularly important for the TECs, whose government contracts for the delivery of training and business support programmes require a partnership approach (LGMB, 1995). The TECs (Local Enterprise Companies [LECs] in Scotland), which were established by government in the late 1980s to implement local training policies and to involve local business in training and business development programmes and wider local economic strategies, make important contributions to the local labour market dimensions of local partnership strategies (LGMB, 1995). The Western Isles and Skye and Lochalsh LEADER project is a local partnership in which two Scottish LECs played a leadership role.

Other public bodies, including police authorities and health authorities, recognise that solutions to the problems posed for them by poverty and exclusion, especially where those problems are concentrated in particular neighbourhoods, require a partnership approach. Such agencies also consider that they bring to local partnerships considerable knowledge and experience of problems associated with exclusion.

The private sector

Business has responded to government's advocacy of partnership both through employer organisations and through the involvement of individual employers. However, the nature of business involvement varies widely, from the largely symbolic to a substantial commitment of resources. Business in the Community, formed to encourage corporate responsibility among business interests, has been a big influence in stimulating business involvement in local partnerships in numerous localities (Roberts et al, 1995).

There are many examples of participation by individual companies in local regeneration partnerships. These range from construction and development companies (especially in partnerships such as City Challenge with substantial resources for physical regeneration and

commercial and housing property development, as in North Tyneside
or Castlemilk for example) to manufacturing and service sector firms
(as in Coventry and Warwickshire, where the initial chair of the
partnership board was the chief executive of Jaguar Cars, one of the
leading local employers).

At a local level, Chambers of Commerce are the main umbrella
bodies for business (especially small and medium-sized firms). There
are a number of instances where Chambers have developed an outward-
looking and proactive role in the local economy and in local
partnerships (eg, the London Enterprise Agency [LENTA] and in
Birmingham), but in other locations Chambers are less active. The
boundaries between the roles in local partnerships of local Chambers,
TECs, and the new Business Link organisations providing local business
support, can also be indistinct. Local Chambers are among the business
partners in the Tyneside and Coventry and Warwickshire Partnerships.

Reasons why employers have a local involvement – including
participation in partnerships – can include both advantages to the
company itself and a more general commitment to the economic and
social prospects of their locality (Coopers and Lybrand/Business in the
Community, undated).

> "Prosperous back streets make prosperous high
> streets." (Marks and Spencer, Employment Depart-
> ment Group, 1995)

> "No business exists in a vacuum. If a community as a
> whole flourishes, the individual members of that
> community tend to flourish too. The more prosperous
> a community is, the more it will buy our goods and
> services. This is mutually beneficial, since the more we
> can improve our financial performance, the more we
> can give back to the community." (Thorn-EMI,
> Employment Department Group, 1995)

This type of commitment has been strongly encouraged by national
government, although an issue of continuing concern has been the
limited willingness of business, especially smaller firms, to adopt this
role (Peck and Tickell, 1995). Individual managers from the private
sector may participate in local partnerships either as a result of
individual motivation or of company policy. A recent study showed the
widespread nature of such 'volunteering', but also the widespread
perception by 'volunteers' of the need for more support from their
companies (Coe, 1995). As well as the direct involvement of individual

business partners, employer participation can take place through the indirect route of business representation on partner bodies such as the TECs.

Private sector organisations and individuals are seen to bring to partnerships resources such as land and money in some cases, and human capital, particularly management skills. Such skills may include development expertise, an ability to put deals together, and clarity in setting goals and objectives. Prominent representatives of business in local partnerships are, however, critical of some elements of the current context of partnership, including limitations of timescales and funding, confused objectives and priorities of local projects, and what is seen as government's piecemeal and uncoordinated approach and unwillingness to give adequate autonomy to local partnerships (Business in the Community, 1994).

There is an increasing recognition by business that community involvement needs to be sustained if it is to bring returns. This is reflected in the growing resourcing by business of community capacity-building. This can be through not-for-profit organisations, such as the Prince of Wales' Business Leaders' Forum or the Civic Trust, which has developed a partnership with private sector firms and the Department of the Environment, Transport and the Regions to offer training and development to community representatives within regeneration partnerships. The Industrial Society runs a similar scheme with the Community Development Foundation (The Industrial Society, 1995).

Trade unions

In contrast to some other EU countries, in the UK trade unions do not play a role in the administration of social protection schemes, nor are they recognised to have a representative status in relation to the interests of all working people rather than just their own members. Trade unions do, however, have an important role to play in combating social exclusion, especially in relation to issues of employment and training. In the UK, the network of Centres for the Unemployed is the main framework through which the trade unions have campaigned locally with and for unemployed people and advised them on benefits, training and other issues.

In many local partnerships trade union representation has not been invited, but examples where trade unions are partners include Coventry and Warwickshire Partnerships, and in the Western Isles and Skye and Lochalsh LEADER project where the Scottish Crofters Union was an important partner.

The Trades Union Congress (TUC) takes the view that all significant social and economic players, including the unions, must have a role in countering exclusion. The main way in which the trade union movement in the UK has responded locally to problems of exclusion is through supporting a network of local Centres for the Unemployed. These centres provide a focus for support and organisation by unemployed workers, and for links with other local activity. On Merseyside, for example, an area of high long-term unemployment, the Centre houses a library, sports centre, children's centre, printing press and recording studio. The TUC recognises that to play their full part, unions must show an ability to represent the interests and support the objectives of groups of people who are not, and sometimes are not likely to be, union members. Because trade unions in the UK are not involved in the administration of social protection schemes, developing ways to campaign with unemployed people and represent their interests is particularly important (Monks, 1995).

Trade unions have a particular role to play in relation to training, and the TUC believes that the market-driven, employer-led voluntary training system in the UK has contributed to a failure to meet the skill needs of the economy. The TUC advocates a new social partnership for training, based in bodies such as TECs, and the need to develop union awareness so that unions could take full advantage of a partnership framework (TUC, 1994).

Voluntary sector

Major voluntary sector agencies have traditionally had an important role in social policy, especially in relation to the needs of specific social groups, such as elderly people or children. Increasingly, such agencies have entered into much closer partnership relationships with local government and the public sector in providing a range of services. They are often involved in local partnerships, although not necessarily as formal partners. Church-based organisations and smaller local voluntary organisations may also be partners in, or have a close involvement with, local partnerships concerned with poverty and exclusion. The partnerships described in Chapter 2 give some indication of the range of voluntary sector involvement.

The voluntary sector in the UK argues that non-statutory and not-for-profit organisations can make an important contribution to local partnerships because of their extensive knowledge and experience in identifying and meeting needs in the community (NCVO and LGMB, 1993). Voluntary organisations argue that they can bring additional resources to partnerships, are innovative in finding new responses to old problems, and are often best able to achieve race and gender equality objectives.

The National Council For Voluntary Organisations (NCVO), the umbrella organisation for the voluntary sector, particularly welcomes the fact that the recent direction of government policy, especially the guidelines for the SRB, encourages more voluntary sector organisations to participate in local regeneration partnerships. The NCVO notes, however, that the participation of voluntary agencies is still partial and patchy, and frequently their involvement can be marginal. It suggests that government should continue to press for greater voluntary (and community) involvement (NCVO, 1995).

The community and community organisations

The direct involvement of the community and community organisations in local partnerships is now seen as a central element of a partnership approach. At the local level, community involvement in partnerships can be through local community organisations (tenants and residents associations, welfare rights or community groups), through local forums representing local community interests in various ways (such as Community Development Trusts [CDTs]), or through individual activists. Different forms and levels of community representation in formal partnership structures are evident in all the partnerships described in Chapter 2, from those associated with national and EU programmes to those resulting from local initiatives.

Although local government claims to be the legitimate voice of the local community as a whole, community organisations can often bring to partnerships a more intimate knowledge and experience of the needs of specific local constituencies and communities. This is vital for informing strategy and policy processes so that local people benefit directly from partnership activities. The Community Development Foundation, one of the main organisations promoting community development in the UK, argues that the community can play a number of important roles in local regeneration partnerships and projects. The community is one of the beneficiaries of partnership activity; community partners are representatives of local opinion; community organisations can help to deliver parts of partnership programmes; and the community can be a long-term partner in the regeneration process (Community Development Foundation, 1995a).

The capacity of local community organisations to contribute to the development of strategies for their areas has been demonstrated in a number of areas.   However, it is recognised that community involvement may also be hampered by a number of factors, from disagreements and tensions within communities and community organisations to the under-resourcing of community organisations, and the lack of familiarity of community partners with the rules, procedures and skills of formal partnership projects.   A number of national organisations, including the Community Development Foundation, the Neighbourhood Initiatives Foundation and the Development Trusts Association, have developed a very important role in sustaining local community involvement and in helping to represent community interests at national level (Community Development Foundation, 1995b; LGMB/Environment Trust, 1995; Macfarlane, 1993; Wilcox, 1994).

As with organisations representing the voluntary sector, community support organisations welcome the greater opportunities for community involvement offered in more recent government programmes, but call for further steps to strengthen this in programmes such as the SRB. These should include better targeting of projects to specific groups including ethnic minorities, women, young people, people with disabilities and the unemployed; procedures to enhance community consultation during the progress of local schemes; a greater role for community organisations as deliverers of projects and attention to the capacity of community groups and organisations to continue after the end of fixed-term initiatives.

An indication of the involvement of different partners in local partnerships is given by analysis of approved bids for funding to the 1995-96 SRB Challenge Fund, which allocated £1.1bn to 201 proposals.   Local authorities were involved in 86% of approved bids and were the lead partner in 53%; TECs in 76%, leading 23%.   The private sector was involved in 83% but led only 7.5%, and the voluntary sector was a partner in 46% but led only 4.5%.

Conclusion

This review has shown that the UK offers many examples of multi-partner local partnerships with multidimensional strategies and action programmes.   Local partnerships typically include partners from the public, private, voluntary and community sectors, and, although much less frequently, from trade unions.   The lead role is, however, most frequently taken by public or quasi-public agencies, local government and TECs or LECs.   While some local partnerships in the UK involve only informal collaboration among local players, many others, especially those associated with major funding programmes, exhibit formal and strong organisational structures distinct from those of partner agencies. Action to combat deprivation, poverty and exclusion in disadvantaged areas makes up important objectives in these partnerships.

However, a central feature of the development of local partnerships in the UK is a focus on urban regeneration – including issues of deprivation and poverty, but also objectives concerning local economic competitiveness and physical renewal. Some local partnerships cover prosperous as well as disadvantaged areas. This is especially the case with those funded by government programmes – the largest and most visible ones – especially City Challenge and the SRB. In this context, the local partnerships supported by the EU's Poverty 3 programme are of distinctive interest as models of local partnership specifically concerned with poverty and exclusion.

The dominant urban regeneration agenda of local partnership in the UK also reflects the relatively low policy priority of rural problems in a highly urbanised country, although the emergence of new programmes such as Rural Challenge indicates an increasing transfer of the partnership philosophy from the urban to the rural context. Here again a distinctive contribution has been made by a European programme, in this case, the LEADER initiative.

The local partnership approach is strongly established in the UK. Chapter 2 will explore, through examples, some of the diversity that currently exists. However, while local partnership seems likely to be an important element of the policy response to problems of poverty and social exclusion for the foreseeable future, a number of problems are also apparent. Many policy makers still suspect that partnership is frequently only skin deep, especially where it reflects an element of compulsion rather than a willing commitment by some partners. How far are the objectives and activities of different partners – including their activities outside as well as within local partnerships – actually reconcilable in common strategies and action plans? Other concerns are with the difficulties and costs of partnership working, especially for less powerful and well-resourced partners, and the frequently limited resources – of money and time – within which local partnerships are expected to make a difference (Stewart and Taylor, 1995). The extent to which local regeneration partnerships can and do prioritise problems of poverty and exclusion is also an issue. Despite provision for monitoring and evaluation being built in to major partnership programmes, it is often not easy to identify the specific contribution of partnership to policy outcomes (Mackintosh, 1992). These and other issues will be explored further in the next chapter, which reviews eight local partnerships in different parts of the UK, and then through three in-depth case studies of local partnership in Part Two.

Chapter 2

Examples of local partnerships

Introduction

This chapter describes eight local partnerships which illustrate important dimensions of the local partnership approach to combating social exclusion in the UK, drawing on evaluations and other documentation produced by and for them. These include partnerships in which initiative has come variously from European programmes, from national initiative and from local and grass roots initiative. The partnerships described are not intended to be 'representative', but they illustrate a range of partnership structures and relationships in different urban and rural contexts, of levels of resourcing, and of achievements. To reflect more recent developments, they include newer partnerships as well as more established ones where a clearer evaluation of outcomes has been made. The description and evaluation of each partnership is based on information available at the time of the research in 1995, and do not reflect any developments since then. The eight partnerships are identified on the map in Figure 1 and summarised in Table 1.

Brownlow Community Trust

Location

Brownlow is a housing estate containing about 9,000 people. It is situated in a predominantly rural area of Northern Ireland not far from the border with the Republic and 25 miles from Belfast. The estate was built in the 1960s as part of a proposed New Town, the product of a major plan for the redevelopment of Belfast and economic expansion within Northern Ireland. However, recession in the 1970s and 1980s meant that the plans were abandoned after the Brownlow estate was built, leaving it in a physically, economically and socially isolated position.

Figure 1: Location of local partnerships in the UK

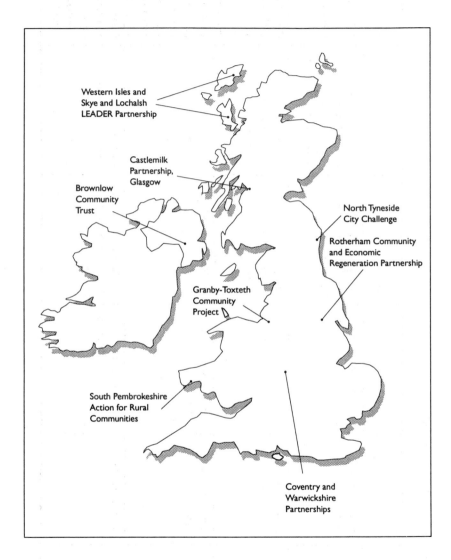

Western Isles and Skye and Lochalsh LEADER Partnership

Castlemilk Partnership, Glasgow

Brownlow Community Trust

North Tyneside City Challenge

Rotherham Community and Economic Regeneration Partnership

Granby-Toxteth Community Project

South Pembrokeshire Action for Rural Communities

Coventry and Warwickshire Partnerships

Table 1: Key features of local partnerships

Partnership	Geographical location	Origins	Funding	Key issues	Partners
Brownlow Community Trust	Urban/peripheral region	Grass roots/ community initiative and EU (Poverty 3)	EU (Poverty 3) to 1994, then Structural Funds and local funding	Poverty, unemployment, housing, health, education, community development, women and children	Public agencies, local community, employer (limited)
Castlemilk Partnership, Glasgow	Urban (conurbation)	Local community, local and central government	Central and local government, private sector	Economic development, housing, environment, education, social improvement	Central government, local public and quasi-public agencies, private sector, local community, voluntary sector
Coventry and Warwickshire Partnerships Ltd	Urban and rural (city region)	Local government, local community in neighbourhood partnerships	SRB Challenge Fund	Economic and social regeneration	Local government, local public and quasi-public agencies, private sector, voluntary sector, community organisations and groups, trade unions
Granby-Toxteth Community Project	Urban (inner city)	Local community/ agencies and EU (Poverty 3)	EU (Poverty 3) to 1994, then national and local funding	Poverty, unemployment, housing, community development, ethnic groups	Central and local government, local community, university, church groups, employers (limited)

Partnership	Geographical location	Origins	Funding	Key issues	Partners
North Tyneside City Challenge Partnership Ltd	Urban (old industrial region)	Local government, local community and UK government (City Challenge)	City Challenge and associated funding	Economic development, physical regeneration, social regeneration	Local government, local public and quasi-public agencies, private sector, local community
Rotherham Community and Economic Regeneration Partnership	Urban and rural coalfield	Local government	Local authority	Employment and economic development, poverty, housing, community development	Local government, local public and quasi-public agencies, national agencies, local community, voluntary sector
South Pembrokeshire Partnership for Action with Rural Communities	Rural	Local/regional partnership and EU (LEADER)	EU: LEADER I and II and matching funding	Rural community development, business development, rural tourism, environmental improvement	Public and quasi-public agencies, community organisations
Western Isles and Skye and Lochalsh LEADER Partnership	Remote rural	Public agencies and EU (LEADER)	EU: LEADER I and II and other public and private funding	Innovative rural development and enterprise, cultural regeneration	Public and quasi-public agencies, farmers' organisations, non-governmental organisations

Origins

The origins of the Brownlow Community Trust (BCT) lie in active community organisation which dates back to the late 1960s and the development of the town itself (Bailey et al, 1995). With the closure of a major employer and a failure to attract further investment, Brownlow has suffered from high and long-term unemployment, leading to population decline and growing crime and vandalism. In 1988, Brownlow community groups published a Greater Brownlow Review, leading to a coordinated effort by community representatives and statutory agencies to develop a common strategy to regenerate Brownlow. This led in due course to a successful funding application to the EU's Poverty 3 programme.

Objectives and activities

As one of the UK 'model' (pilot) actions of the Poverty 3 programme, the remit and objectives of BCT reflected the programme's principles of partnership, participation and multidimensionality. The strategy and activity plan developed by the Trust focused on the needs of three main social groups: women, children and the unemployed. BCT supported and resourced activity and projects for all these groups. Initiatives included a Brownlow Women's Forum, a Children's Policy Forum and a health project. The Trust attempted to build community infrastructure within Brownlow, to focus the policies of public agencies, and to promote more effective working between agencies and the community.

Funding

Funding of approximately £2.2m was obtained for a five-year period from 1989 to 1994 through the Poverty 3 programme. A separate economic development fund was set up with funding from the Department of the Environment and the Investment Fund for Ireland to promote business investment.

Partners

The BCT management board was made up primarily of representatives of statutory agencies and community interests. Agency representation included the health, education, housing and economic development agencies and the local authority. The trust invested considerable resources in ensuring that different elements of the community were represented, although this continued to be a source of some tension. Representation was both from community organisations and by election from different parts of the estate.   Due to the limited number of significant local employers and the existence of a separate economic development agency the private sector was under-represented.   There was strong representation of women on the management board on the 'community side' and in the project team.

Present status

Although Poverty 3 funding has since terminated, BCT helped to create a new administrative culture in the area, with greater interagency collaboration and consultation with local people.   Many of the initiatives developed and facilitated, especially those concerned with women's employment, have continued after the termination of the Poverty 3 partnership (Gaffikin and Morrissey, 1995).   A further three years of funding from the EU Structural Funds has been secured, with matching funding from the local authority and other public agencies. This funding, although only totalling about £250,000 per year, is being used to maintain BCT as a community development agency on a wider basis serving the area of the original Craigavon New Town.

Assessment

The local partnership established by the BCT has enabled it to develop an innovative and multidimensional approach to social policy issues in a highly marginalised and excluded area.   Considerable success has been achieved in involving and empowering excluded groups (even though significant tensions between sections of the community remained, for example, over the issue of the response that the Trust should make to the needs of a traveller 'community').   BCT can also claim considerable success in making statutory agencies much more aware of local needs, even though responsibility for key issues, such as housing, did not lie with the trust, and consequently BCT was not always able to secure policy actions which it considered desirable.   In particular, the care taken to involve women in the trust's structure and processes enabled BCT to recognise the ways in which gender discrimination effects women in deprived communities, and action for women has been a priority within the trust's activity programme.   However, the level of resources available to the trust, though significant, did not enable it to have a major effect on the material conditions of life of Brownlow's inhabitants.   In particular, the allocation of economic development responsibilities to a separate agency (which itself achieved only limited impact) meant that the material impact of the partnership on social exclusion was restricted.

The Castlemilk Partnership, Glasgow

Location

The city of Glasgow in central Scotland provides an example of several local urban anti-poverty partnerships. Glasgow has several large peripheral housing estates which have become major concentrations of poverty and social exclusion, with different experiences of economic and social regeneration initiatives. In the Drumchapel area, initiative came largely from local government, with the establishment in 1989 of Drumchapel Opportunities, an employment, training and neighbourhood regeneration initiative which emphasises the economic empowerment of local residents. In the Easterhouse and East End areas there have been similar though less prominent initiatives. A further initiative has been located on Castlemilk, a large peripheral estate on the southern edge of Glasgow, whose population has halved from a high point of 37,000 in 1971.

Origins

The Castlemilk Partnership was established in 1988 by the Scottish Office as an Urban Partnership Area, on the base of an earlier small-scale local initiative with a strong community network. At the outset of the partnership the Castlemilk estate was characterised by low average household incomes, high unemployment, low educational and skill levels, poor and unpopular housing, a degraded environment, poor private services and high demand for public services, and a poor image.

Objectives and activities

The main issue facing the partnership has been to arrest population decline and, in its words, "to create in Castlemilk a well-functioning suburb, better integrated with the Glasgow conurbation but with more local jobs and services" (O'Toole et al, 1995). Large-scale housing and environmental renovation and diversification has been accompanied by training and employment projects and social and community initiatives. Anti-poverty initiatives have been one element of this strategy, especially through initiatives to improve public services and reduce their cost to poor people.

Funding

The partnership does not have a fixed overall budget, but about £150m of public capital expenditure has been invested during the first five years, 75% of it on housing. The £110m public housing spend has been accompanied by £20m private investment.

Partners

The partnership has membership drawn from the public, non-statutory and private sectors. Public partners include the representatives nominated by the Scottish Office, Strathclyde Regional and Glasgow District Councils, the Employment Service, the Greater Glasgow Health Board and Glasgow Development Agency. The private sector is involved through the Castlemilk Business Support Group. The partnership is not a legally constituted body, but a committee of independent organisations which seeks to influence the policies of its members.

A partnership group guides decision making, assisted by an administrative partnership team. Considerable efforts have been made to involve the community in both strategy development and implementation.

Defining features of the partnership are intended to be its flexibility, responsiveness to local concerns and ability to take on new issues as they emerge.

Present status

Achievement of the objectives of the partnership is seen to be a long-term process which will continue to need levels of public and private investment at least as large as those of the first five years. A new six-year housing investment programme starting in 1994 is a major step in this direction. The second phase of the partnership is placing greater emphasis on smaller projects with community involvement as well as large-scale investment programmes. Forward planning is taking place for 'exit' – the winding up of the current partnership arrangement and the establishment of 'successor bodies', including more effective community involvement.

Assessment

The interim evaluation of the first phase of the partnership (O'Toole et al, 1995) suggested there have been significant achievements in housing and in raising skill levels, and in collaboration between professionals and with the community in education, health and community care. Resources expended elsewhere would be unlikely to have produced equivalent results without the catalytic effects of partnership. However, the impact on jobs has been limited. Consequently, while some of the consequences of poverty have been alleviated, it may be beyond the power of the Castlemilk local partnership to reduce poverty significantly. Local community businesses have been supported by a local development agency, but the community withdrew from participation in this because of its perceived lack of accountability to local people (Stewart and Taylor, 1995).

It is considered that partnership working has been an important learning experience in multi-agency cooperation between the government and the community and between departments and professions within government. This has been due to high level political commitment by leading stakeholders, and resource support. However, the role of the private sector in partnership activity has been more limited to objectives close to its direct interests, such as training, rather than the broader strategy.

The community has been closely involved in the partnership, but so far there is little sign of long-term community empowerment, partly because of the tension between allowing time for community involvement and the rapid delivery of major investment programmes.

Coventry and Warwickshire Partnerships Limited

Location

Coventry is a major manufacturing city in the English Midlands, whose traditional industries have been a microcosm of the broader West Midlands regional economy based on the car industry and other manufacturing and basic industries. The economy of the surrounding county of Warwickshire is closely linked to that of Coventry by travel to work patterns and interfirm linkages. The decline of traditional industries has impacted particularly on certain social groups and neighbourhoods.

Origins

In Coventry and Warwickshire there is a long history of liaison between local agencies in promoting economic development, despite important differences of perspective. There is also a tradition of community-based organisation and activity in certain local communities. Recently, the urgency of economic and social regeneration has promoted the development of a much stronger partnership framework both between public agencies and with business and other interests, through the formation of Coventry and Warwickshire Partnerships Ltd (CWP).

Objectives and activities

The overall aim of CWP is to develop an economic regeneration strategy to "improve the quality of life, prosperity and wealth of the people of Coventry and Warwickshire" (Coventry and Warwickshire Partnerships Ltd, 1995). A total of 10 strategic objectives have been identified and grouped into four action programmes concerned with physical regeneration, business development, human and social development, and advocacy on behalf of the area. Action to tackle poverty and exclusion constitutes one part of this broad economic and social regeneration agenda.

Funding

The partnership framework helps to draw together and coordinate the activity and investment of different partners, but the partnership has also been successful in obtaining substantial resources (£22.5m) from the government's SRB Challenge Fund.

Partners

The partnership brings together public, private, voluntary and community partners. Individual members are nominated by partner organisations, but in the initial stage of the partnership contacts between a few key individuals were important in creating the basis of trust to establish it. The founding members were Coventry City Council, Warwickshire County Council, the local TEC and Coventry and Warwickshire Chamber of Commerce and Industry. Further members include the second tier district councils in Warwickshire, the two local universities (Coventry and Warwick) and other higher education institutions, manufacturing and service sector businesses, voluntary and community organisations and trade unions. The partnership has a two-tier structure with a main board (on which the main stakeholders are represented) and executive committee responsible for overall strategy. Of the 25 members of the board (early 1995) three were women, of whom two were from the voluntary sector and one was from higher education, although none of the women had places on the executive committee. There was one representative of ethnic minority organisations. Below the main decision-making level, specific areas of activity are the responsibility of either subsidiary companies/partnerships or of partner organisations themselves. A small project team has been established.

Present status

The partnership has developed rapidly and now has 59 organisations in membership. A priority is to find ways to actively involve the range of member organisations, and also to communicate with local communities and the wider public.

The resources made available from the SRB are enabling the partnership to take a considerable step forward towards implementing strategic objectives, through projects ranging from advanced technology and engineering competitiveness to rural transport and social and physical regeneration in inner and outer urban areas in different parts of the region. At the same time, further resources are being sought both from the SRB and from European Union programmes and initiatives.

Assessment

CWP illustrates some of the ways in which the partnership approach is currently developing in the UK, influenced by programmes such as the SRB. The partnership has a formal framework with legal status. There is a wide range of partners, including trade unions and local community interests, although business representation is strongest on the main partnership board. The partnership brings together different local authorities to undertake regeneration at a subregional level. The partnership has a wide remit, ranging from business development and industrial competitiveness to problems of deprivation and exclusion. If it can continue to harness the contributions of the numerous partners effectively it will attract wide interest from other areas. This partnership is discussed in more detail in Chapter 5.

Granby-Toxteth Community Project

Location

Granby-Toxteth Community Project (GTCP) was situated in an inner-city district of Liverpool with a large and long-established ethnic minority population. It remains one of the poorest areas of the city with a history of antagonism between and within black, ethnic and white local communities, with class, gender and racial dimensions, despite 20 years of programmes and initiatives to combat deprivation and poverty.

Origins

GTCP was one of the UK model actions funded by the EU's Poverty 3 programme, 1989-94. The origins of the Poverty 3 partnership lie in the long history of regeneration initiatives and community activism in the area.

Objectives and activities

The strategy of the Granby-Toxteth partnership focused on enabling local people to benefit from urban regeneration schemes being undertaken by central and local government, both by helping to enable the local community to participate in decision making, and by local labour and training schemes. The partnership also aimed to provide a community development resource for the locality, for example, through a project to encourage local people to claim state benefits due to them and a community newspaper.

Funding

The project was funded through the Poverty 3 programme, with co-funding from local regeneration agencies responsible to central government and other agencies. An objective of the project was to use the Poverty 3 funding to identify and lever in other sources of funding for community organisations and initiatives.

Partners

GTCP brought together a range of partners including central and local government, community organisations, the local university, religious organisations and, less centrally, the private sector. The central and local government representatives saw themselves as lead partners; the involvement of other public and voluntary organisations was less consistent. Community representation was through three black and Afro-Asian Caribbean organisations, although there was a view from other sections of the community that wider representation of social groups, including single parents and the unemployed, might have been desirable.

Present status

GTCP developed an exit strategy for the period after Poverty 3 funding ended, which enabled many of its more successful initiatives to be taken over by a development trust. The lead agency of the trust was the government-supported Granby-Toxteth Task Force but also involved were the local authority and Liverpool Council for Voluntary Services. This was associated with a more concerted approach to community involvement covering a wider geographical area, and a broadening of the scope of activity to include greater priority for economic development. This in turn was helped by the granting of EU Structural Funds Objective 1 status to Merseyside.

Assessment

Liverpool has been the scene of long-standing conflicts between central and local government, between local public authorities and sections of the community, especially some black and ethnic groups, and within the diverse ethnic community (Moore, 1997). Some of the more important lessons from the Granby-Toxteth partnership concern the barriers which such conflicts present to effective local partnership against social exclusion. These included problems of gender and racial 'balance' within the partnership and coordination of policy priorities between agencies and with the community sector. As a result, the partnership encountered continual problems in delivering a coherent work programme and fully utilising the available funding (House of Lords, 1994). However, the partnership has now entered a new phase, and the experience of the Poverty 3 project may have helped to induce greater flexibility in public agencies while making community interests more aware of the constraints under which the public sector works.

North Tyneside City Challenge Partnership

Location

North Tyneside lies at the mouth of the river Tyne in North East England, in an area of long-term and high unemployment caused by the decline of traditional industries such as coalmining and shipbuilding. Within the area are several large and rundown housing estates, including the Meadowell estate which was the scene of serious rioting in 1991.

Origins

There is a long history of regeneration projects and programmes in North East England and on Tyneside. In the 1970s, community development projects in both Newcastle and Tyneside were part of an experimental UK government programme of localised anti-poverty initiatives. In the 1980s, an urban development corporation was set up to redevelop the rundown waterfront area of North Tyneside, and the City Challenge area is now adjacent to this. The City Challenge proposal was led by the local authority, North Tyneside Metropolitan Borough Council, but the successful bid also included community initiatives on the Meadowell estate, where community leaders had developed plans for renewal in the wake of the 1991 disturbances.

Objectives and activities

North Tyneside City Challenge Partnership (NTCCP) is a major urban regeneration project, with a five-year strategy and action plan involving integrated physical, economic and social regeneration, in which tackling poverty, unemployment and exclusion are seen as priorities. The strategy of the partnership is seek to encourage the entrepreneurial activity of local people and their participation in community life. The action plan of the partnership includes a number of large 'flagship' projects concerned with the renewal of industrial, commercial and residential areas, and many other projects and initiatives to increase employment, develop industry and commerce, raise skills levels, improve the environment, reduce crime and improve community facilities.

Funding

During the five years of its operation from 1993 to 1998, NTCCP can draw on £37.5m of City Challenge funds, largely channelled through the local authority. Most of the projects which the partnership is undertaking are co-funded by other partners, so the programme draws on substantial further public money and private investment.

Partners

NTCCP is a limited company. It is run by a board of directors with 20 members grouped into five 'forums' representing business, housing, an 'economic assembly', including the TEC, English Partnerships, the Development Corporation and the police, a community forum and local government interests. The participation of women as directors has been almost exclusively confined to the community sector, but in this forum the representation has been predominantly by women. The area has only an extremely small ethnic minority population and there are no ethnic minority members on the board. Seven members of the board form the executive committee, and a partnership team of 10 people is responsible for implementing the action plan.

Most directors are nominated by partner organisations, although some serve on the basis of personal expertise and contacts rather than in a representative role. Community representation is organised on an area basis from each of the main housing estates, increasingly by election from local community forums which the partnership has supported to help represent the views of local people, along with community development trusts to implement some of the community projects.

Present status

In 1995/96 the five-year action plan was about half way towards completion.

Assessment

In North Tyneside, the City Challenge partnership has encouraged a wider partnership approach to local regeneration than earlier government programmes. While the intention of the government was that City Challenge should be business led, in North Tyneside it has offered a more prominent role to the local authority in particular.

NTCCP has made rapid progress in developing effective partnership working among public agencies and with the private sector interests represented. Active community involvement, however, remains relatively restricted.

The investment and projects undertaken by the partnership are having a major effect in modernising important elements of the industrial, commercial and housing infrastructure. However, partners remain cautious about the ability of the partnership to tackle poverty, partly because of contributory factors outside the control of local players. The partnership is responsible for a considerable investment programme, but its experience so far indicates that in areas of severe deprivation, even strong local partnerships with significant resources may only be able to have a limited impact on employment and hence on poverty and exclusion.

This partnership is discussed more fully in Chapter 3.

Rotherham Community and Economic Regeneration Partnership

Location

The town of Rotherham in South Yorkshire, and the surrounding rural areas, have been badly affected by the rapid decline of the coalmining and steel industries. Between the late 1970s and the early 1990s nearly 20,000 jobs were lost in these two industries. Male unemployment now stands at more than 20% and some communities have lost their whole economic raison d'être.

Origins

In response to rising unemployment and poverty the local authority, Rotherham Metropolitan Borough Council has played a leading role in developing anti-poverty and economic and community regeneration initiatives in partnership with other local agencies.

The initiative has been strongly led by the authority's Labour council, key members of which are also active in the National Local Government Forum Against Poverty. The local authority is also an active member of the Coalfields Communities Campaign which was influential in the European Community's decision to introduce the RECHAR programme for aid to coalfields.

Objectives and activities

The initiative involves both a strong corporate anti-poverty strategy within the local authority, and partnership between the local authority, local communities and other agencies in community and economic regeneration.

Within the local authority, anti-poverty strategy has been strengthened by reviewing priorities and targeting resources, so that 'who gets what' is closer to 'who needs what'. This has included focusing resources on a multi-agency basis in the most disadvantaged communities, advice on benefits for old and young people and the unemployed, and a 'leisure card' offering discounts at a range of facilities to those on benefits.

The Rotherham Community and Economic Regeneration strategy funds regeneration projects and supports community development. A major initiative is in South Rotherham, where a bottom-up partnership strategy is being developed to secure external funding for the regeneration of an area which has suffered particularly from the decline of coalmining. The Eastwell/Oakwood partnership has been formed to generate resources for a highly deprived area of the town of Rotherham (Chester-Kadwell et al, 1995).

Funding

The Rotherham Community and Economic Regeneration strategy has a budget of £2.5m. Funding for the South Rotherham programme is being sought from the Rural Development Commission. The Eastwood/Oakwell partnership has presented a bid for £21m to the SRB Challenge Fund for a five-year regeneration programme.

Partners

The South Rotherham Community and Economic Regeneration Partnership includes representatives from the local authority, the health authority, the police, the local TEC, local parish councils, many organisations from the local voluntary sector and various community organisations. The Eastwell/Oakwood partnership is led by the local authority and the TEC, but also includes housing associations and developers, tenants groups, black and Asian organisations and other interests. Equal opportunity issues are a priority for the local authority, which has a strong social policy team (Rotherham Metropolitan

Borough Council, 1995), and this is reflected in the Rotherham Community and Economic Regeneration strategy.

Present status

The framework of partnership in Rotherham includes both formal and more informal partnership arrangements, relating to a range of linked anti-poverty and regeneration initiatives and the search for external funding. At the time of this research the framework was, however, in a state of active development.

Assessment

The rapid development in Rotherham of local partnership frameworks to combat poverty and deprivation and promote regeneration is a leading example of current trends within many localities in the UK, where local authorities are seeking to gain a share of the opportunities for funding offered by highly competitive and resource-limited national programmes, and to promote and support grass roots initiative and activity, and find positive ways of linking economic and social policy at the local level.

South Pembrokeshire Partnership for Action with Rural Communities

Location

South Pembrokeshire is an area of mainly small rural communities in the south west of Wales. The area has traditionally been regarded as relatively prosperous within the Welsh context, but more recently it has suffered from the decline of agriculture and other local industries, emigration of young people and a marked ageing of the population.

Origins

The South Pembrokeshire Partnership for Action with Rural Communities (SPARC) was established in 1992 within the framework of the EU's LEADER I Initiative. It built upon the earlier Taff and Cleddau Rural Initiative funded by the Welsh Development Agency. Both initiatives emphasised a strongly 'bottom-up' approach to sustainable rural development involving all sections of the community in integrated strategies for economic, social, environmental and cultural renewal.

Objectives and activities

SPARC aimed to be a "people's partnership which has an explicit focus on the development of communities, by providing them with the means to improve their social relationships, economic circumstances and the environment in which they live, and by fostering the confidence within them *as communities* to be able to bring about these actions themselves" (Midmore et al, 1995). Consequently, the programme has focused on community appraisals and relatively small-scale projects, especially supporting the development of local businesses and promoting environmentally sensitive rural tourism to encourage diversification out of agriculture.

Funding

The aim of SPARC was to use LEADER resources to generate locally added value and lever in additional public and private investment. Multiple funding was seen as important in ensuring that the project was not 'captured' by a single agency, and was able to promote the interests of local people even when these conflicted with some funders' priorities.

Partners

The SPARC programme has been implemented through partnership between communities, funding agencies, advisory bodies and local authorities. Community involvement was built principally on the community associations supported by the Taff and Cleddau Rural Initiative. Community representatives elected half the members of the management council. A project team was led by a coordinator with project officers responsible for specific aspects of the programme. A feature of the partnership was a sustained attempt to facilitate community involvement through promoting community associations and community appraisals and plans. This achieved considerable success, but in some areas active involvement was difficult to secure and tensions arose between the objective of empowering communities and the desire to get results.

Present status

Together, the Taff and Cleddau and SPARC Initiatives represent a sustained, six-year initiative to build local partnership and establish a network of local community associations concerned to promote development.   The main players remained committed to continued partnership at the end of the LEADER I project, and the local partnership framework has now progressed to a further phase, in which new funding from LEADER II is being complemented by support from the Structural Funds under the Rural Wales Objective 5b Programme (SPARC, 1996).

Assessment

SPARC and its predecessor, the Taff and Cleddau Rural Initiative, achieved a good deal in involving relatively large numbers of people and communities in developing and implementing plans for their areas, and bringing together staff and resources from a range of partners. The partnership was relatively well resourced and so was able to provide a much higher level of technical support for community initiatives than is usual. Even so, the experience of SPARC illustrates the difficulties of allowing time for genuine community involvement in local partnership to develop and providing evidence of programme and project achievements to encourage continued interest. The continuation of local initiative within a partnership framework supported both by LEADER II and Rural Wales Objective 5b Programme is particularly important in that the 5b Programme itself has been considerably shaped by the lessons of LEADER I local partnerships, especially SPARC.

Western Isles and Skye and Lochalsh LEADER Partnership

Location

The Western Isles and Skye and Lochalsh are situated in the remote north west of the Scottish Highlands and Islands. The area has remained largely peripheral to the major processes of urban industrial growth which have transformed other regions, and has suffered a long history of depopulation and out-migration as a result of the marginal nature of the local economy.

Origins

Prior to the LEADER programme, development initiatives in the area had included support from the Highlands and Islands Development Board and EU-funded Integrated Development Programmes in both the Western Isles and Skye. The direct origin of the Western Isles and Skye and Lochalsh (WISL) LEADER Partnership lay in initial collaboration between the two LECs in the area, Western Isles Enterprise (WIE) and Skye and Lochalsh Enterprise (SLE). Support for a LEADER bid was also forthcoming from the Western Isles Islands Council (WIIC) and Highland Regional Council (HRC). The early involvement of two key non-governmental organisations (NGOs), Comunn na Gaidhlig, the Gaelic language agency, and the Scottish Crofters Union, was also important, especially in contributing to the social and cultural dimensions of the LEADER proposal.

Objectives and activities

The philosophy of the LEADER I programme was that local people are the principal assets of rural areas, because of their ability to identify what forms of development are best suited to their environment, culture, working traditions and skills. The WISL LEADER Partnership adapted this philosophy to the local area, through emphasising the restoration of confidence in the area's unique cultural heritage, and using this as a springboard for development based on the area's identity. In addition, local people were encouraged to come forward with their own ideas and were then helped to turn these into projects. These activities and projects covered a wide spectrum, including tourism, crafts and agricultural marketing (WISL LEADER, 1991).

Funding

The WISL LEADER programme received an allocation of £1.4m from the EC over about two years between 1992 and 1994. Together with matching public and private funding, it was anticipated that this would produce a total expenditure of £3.3m. In practice this figure was easily exceeded, with actual global expenditure of more than £4.9m, due to much higher leverage than expected. Co-funding was a feature of many of the projects supported by the partnership.

Partners

The core of the partnership consisted of the two LECs (WIE and SLE), the two local authorities (WIIC and HRC), Comunn na Gaidhlig and the Scottish Crofters Union, each of whom nominated two representatives to the partnership.   LEADER groups were then developed in the two main areas and these included representatives from a number of other organisations, especially higher education institutions, tourism and environmental agencies.   An important role was played by a project coordinator and project team, which included three field officers located in different parts of the area, and a network of part-time animators whose role was to stimulate ideas among local people and then help work these up into projects.   The project coordinator and two of the three field officers in the project team were women, but in contrast nearly all the party agency representatives were men.

Many of the individual projects were themselves developed and implemented on a partnership basis. In all more than 220 projects were implemented despite initial delays in the release of the LEADER funds.

Present status

The LEADER I programme has now terminated but its success has encouraged the agencies involved to remain together and develop a successful follow-up LEADER II project.

Assessment

The WISL LEADER programme achieved considerable success in stimulating local bottom-up development initiatives and initiating a shift away from a local dependency culture. It succeeded in building partnership between local agencies and, through the project team, developing efficient and user-friendly ways of working. However, local communities were not directly involved in the partnership structure and the role of local animators as a link between the partnership and local communities only worked well in certain areas. One measure of the success of the local partnership is the high levels of matching funding attracted from both public and private sources, in comparison to other local LEADER projects.

This local partnership is discussed further in Chapter 4.

Conclusion

This review of the evolution of the local partnership approach to problems of social exclusion in the UK, and the perspectives of different partners in Chapter 1 has indicated a number of important policy issues. Although the ethos and practice of partnership appears firmly established in the UK, there are doubts about the strength of local partnership, and the depth of partner commitment. The broad urban or rural regeneration focus of local policy in the UK may not prioritise policy objectives related to tackling poverty and exclusion.

The examples of local partnership described above raise further and more focused questions. The most important of these are summarised below:

- In any local partnership, the position and influence of different partners is unlikely to be equal. Partnerships have adopted a variety of different structures and working practices and processes to represent partner interests. However, there are strong indications that it is easier to develop partnership between formal organisations (particularly among public agencies but also between the public and private sectors) than with community organisations or excluded social groups.

- The position of women and ethnic groups within local partnerships, and of equal opportunity objectives within partnership strategies and programmes, is a particular issue on which the partnerships described offer widely differing experiences.

- The geographical scale and population base of local partnerships varies considerably. Some partnerships seek to reflect factors such as the regional or subregional scale of local labour markets, while others are more tightly focused on districts of towns and cities or rural social and cultural communities. The scale of the partnership's geographical and population base can have important implications for developing effective partnership.

- The timescales within which local partnerships funded by major national or EU programmes are expected to achieve results is short – mostly four or five years. This may make community involvement much more difficult. It also means that securing the future financial base of the partnership beyond a particular funding source is a crucial issue. The examples discussed include a number of successful experiences in this respect.

- The resources available to local partnerships from national and EU programmes are also severely limited, and, as Chapter 1 suggested, do not match the severity of the problems of poverty and exclusion currently being experienced in the UK. Many more local partnership structures are now being established across the country, but many of these are unlikely to receive significant national or European funding under current arrangements.

- Local partnerships which have had access to significant financial resources have undertaken ambitious programmes of economic and physical regeneration, with accompanying labour market and social initiatives and implications. However, even such well-resourced local partnerships may well only be able to bring partial solutions to deep-seated problems of poverty and exclusion.

The following section explores these and other issues about the effectiveness of local partnerships in combating poverty and exclusion through detailed case studies of three of the partnerships presented in this chapter.

Part Two: Partnership at the local level

Introduction: the three case studies

The case studies are intended to provide detailed examples of how partnerships work in practice, and especially to explore the perspectives and contributions of different partners and stakeholders.

As the case studies are limited to three, they cannot be regarded as fully representative of local partnership in the UK. Nevertheless the three case studies have been selected to illustrate partnerships with different origins – European programmes, national programmes and more local initiative – and different structures and relationships between public agencies, employers, trade unions and the voluntary and community sectors, including different levels of resourcing and financial arrangements. They reflect experience in rural as well as urban-industrial areas, and have been chosen because of the lessons they provide in the context of the research. The case studies (which are based on research undertaken in 1995, and do not reflect events since then), draw on in-depth interviews of representatives of partner agencies, members of the partnership's project team, local community organisations and those involved in projects and initiatives supported by the partnership. They also draw on secondary material including documentation provided by the partnerships.

Each case study has three main parts. An initial section describes the background, structure, remit and objectives and resources of the partnership. The second section is concerned with how the partnership works in practice. It presents the views of partners and stakeholders on the success of the partnership in representing their different interests, in harnessing the commitment, skills and resources of partners around an agreed strategy and action plan, and in dealing with problems and conflicts. The final section assesses the impact of the partnership, including the impact of partnership working on partner agencies and on the wider policy process, and the contribution made to combating social exclusion.

Chapter 3

North Tyneside City Challenge Partnership Ltd

Background

North Tyneside lies at the mouth of the river Tyne in North East England, in an area of long-term high unemployment caused by the decline of traditional industries such as coalmining and shipbuilding. North Tyneside City Challenge Partnership Ltd (NTCCP) is a major urban regeneration project, funded by the UK government's City Challenge programme. The five-year strategy of NTCCP involves integrated physical, economic and social regeneration, in which tackling poverty, unemployment and social exclusion are part of a comprehensive approach to regeneration.

The City Challenge area includes parts of the towns of Wallsend and North Shields, and also several large housing estates. One of these is Meadowell, a particularly rundown estate which was the scene of serious rioting and disturbances in 1991. NTCCP has encouraged the formation of community forums on these estates to help represent the views of local people, and of community development trusts to implement some of the community projects. The Meadowell Forum and Community Development Trust are the most established of these.

Context and origins

Tyneside's economic problems – high unemployment and the collapse of traditional industries – are characteristic of many of the old coalmining, shipbuilding and heavy engineering industrial regions of the UK which are the product of what has been called 'carboniferous capitalism'. In the 1920s these industries directly employed about one third of the Tyneside workforce, but as these have declined the area has not fully shared in the development of more modern manufacturing industries. Industrial decline has been fairly constant since the 1960s with the last shipyard closing in 1993.

With a population of 195,000, North Tyneside includes prosperous coastal and rural areas as well as the depressed urban industrial area along the River Tyne. Nonetheless, the borough ranks 51st out of 336 authorities on the main national index of deprivation. Particular indices on which the area scores poorly are numbers of people on income support, unemployment (especially long-term), children in low income households, derelict land, poor housing and lack of car ownership. In the City Challenge partnership area, the unemployment rate of more than 15% in the early 1990s was well above the national average and has since risen while the national rate has declined. In Meadowell it is estimated at 40%. The economic activity rate for women is particularly low and the number of women in full-time employment even lower. Educational attainment is also low, and the lack of job prospects is reflected in a marked disinterest in training opportunities. Surveys show that residents in areas like Meadowell are dissatisfied with their local environment and community facilities and think that the area has a poor image. There is particular concern about the crime and vandalism, particularly by young males, for which the area has a reputation following the 1991 disturbances. While local residents, especially women, have been active in community organisations, many people have low expectations of the value of getting involved in community activity.

There is a long history of regional and urban economic and social regeneration programmes and projects in North East England. Regional policies have encouraged inward investment since the 1930s, and strong regional lobbying groups representing both business and public authorities have grown up to seek to influence policies in both London and Brussels. In the 1970s community development projects in both North Tyneside and Newcastle were part of a UK government programme of experimental localised anti-poverty initiatives which were precursors of the successive European Poverty Programmes. In the 1980s an urban development corporation was set up to redevelop the riverside areas in Tyne and Wear, including the rundown waterfront area of North Tyneside; the City Challenge partnership area is adjacent to this. The City Challenge proposal was led by the local authority, North Tyneside Metropolitan Borough Council, but the successful bid also drew upon community proposals for the Meadowell estate, where activists had developed plans for renewal in the wake of the 1991 disturbances.

Partnership structure

City Challenge was the major UK government urban regeneration programme of the early 1990s, preceding the current SRB. Launched in 1991-92, £1.2bn was allocated to a series of five-year local projects which had been successful in a competitive bidding process for funding. While competitive bidding for limited resources meant that in the past many areas recognised by government to be suffering from multiple deprivation did not receive funding, many of these City Challenge projects included areas of spatially concentrated poverty and social exclusion. The City Challenge programme is committed to a business-led concept of urban regeneration, but offers more space for local government and local communities than previous programmes.

North Tyneside City Challenge is a limited company. It is run by a board of directors with 20 members grouped into five 'forums': four each from a business forum, a housing forum, a community forum, an economic assembly, and four from the local authority. Figure 2 illustrates its structure. At the time of the research, the board was chaired by a member of the business forum. The local authority members were the leader and deputy leader of the Council, the leader of the opposition group, and the authority's executive director. The business forum brings in major local employers and was soon to include the Tyne and Wear Chamber of Commerce. The housing forum included members from tenants associations alongside housing associations and homebuilders groups. The economic assembly was in operation before the City Challenge partnership was established. As part of the local authority's economic development function, it included representatives from the local TEC, English Partnerships, Tyne and Wear Development Corporation and Northumbria police. The community forum included representatives from each of the four main residential areas (including Meadowell). Three of the four community forum members were women, but all the other board members were men.

Most of the board members were nominated when the bid for City Challenge funding was made. As a result of subsequent changes, some community representatives were then elected via local community forums. Some partners had instituted effective procedures for reporting back on partnership activity: the local authority, for example, has both political and administrative reporting mechanisms through committee and officer structures. However, in other cases, including those where individuals were nominated as much for their personal expertise as to take a representative role, reporting procedures were more informal and more limited.

The board, which meets bi-monthly, is responsible for developing the partnership's strategy and action plan, developing partnership working relationships, approving the use of funds and monitoring performance. Seven members of the board, including the chair, one member from each of the housing, business and economic forums and from the local authority, and two community representatives (both women), formed an executive group. This meets monthly or more frequently and is responsible for prioritising projects, adjusting the programme from year to year and so on.

A chief executive and team undertakes the work of the partnership, reporting to the board and executive group. The team is made up of a programme manager, a monitoring officer, four project officers and three support staff. At the time of the research, 7 of the 10 members of the partnership team were women, but the chief executive was a man. Regular meetings were held with the community forum, and there were special review and monitoring groups with local authority officers. Project teams were established to manage specific projects.

The partnership has a close working relationship with the local authority, through the Council's Policy and Resources Committee, which approves the action programme and sets the framework for the local authority's financial contribution. The Council then adopts an arm's length approach to the implementation of the programme.

Objectives and activities

The objectives and activities of the partnership take the form of a 'vision', a strategy, and a five-year programme of projects (North Tyneside City Challenge Partnership Ltd, 1993; 1994). The vision statement of the partnership commits it to three goals:

- to strengthen the local economy, and, by so doing, increase the opportunities for residents both in the City Challenge area and across the community;

- to deepen the aspirations of local people, to generate entrepreneurial activity, active citizenship and a spirit of community;

- to widen the horizons of residents through creating new jobs, a cleaner environment, choice in housing and high quality local services.

Figure 2: Structure of the North Tyneside City Challenge Partnership

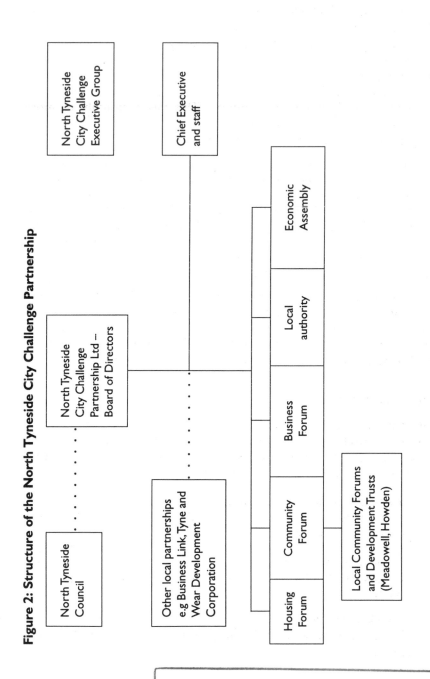

The primary emphasis of the partnership is on economic development and entrepreneurship as a strategy to counter exclusion and deprivation. It is argued that:

> ... stubborn unemployment, poverty and urban decay have combined to damage community spirit and dampen individual aspiration. For years, many local people have relied on large employers, lived in inadequate housing, in communities where both facilities and participation are limited. North Tyneside City Challenge promotes a new vision where local people are encouraged as entrepreneurs and motivated to participate in the life of their communities. (NTCCP, 1993)

This vision is translated into 10 strategic objectives, within each of which a number of operational objectives provide the framework for specific projects. These 10 objectives are to:

- increase employment
- develop industry and commerce
- raise skill levels
- enable business
- improve housing
- improve the environment
- reduce crime
- improve leisure facilities
- develop communities
- improve health.

Among the 'flagship' projects which are vital to the achievement of different objectives are major infrastructural and environmental improvements to key industrial areas, the Riverside Training Centre close to the Meadowell estate and to the Royal Quays development by the Tyne and Wear Development Corporation, and the redevelopment of Union Square in the centre of North Shields for combined office, housing and retail use.

During its five years of operation (1993-98) the partnership intends to achieve a number of targets through the projects undertaken under each objective. These include quantified targets for leverage of private sector investment, housing completions, jobs created and preserved, land reclaimed, new business and commercial floorspace developed, new business start-ups and weeks of training delivered. However, key events such as the closure of the Swan Hunter Shipyard made the partnership increasingly aware of the extent to which its ability to achieve these targets is dependent on private economic decisions and government policies beyond its control. As a consequence, some of the targets have been modified as part of the annual review of the action programme.

Funding

During the five years of its operation from 1993 to 1998, North Tyneside City Challenge Partnership draws on £37.5m of City Challenge funds, largely channelled through the local authority by means of the City Challenge Local Authority Grant. However, most of the projects which the partnership has undertaken are co-funded by other partners, so the programme draws on substantial further public funds and on private investment. It was initially anticipated that £161.8m of private sector investment would be levered in, and there would be £43.7m additional public funding (from other local authority sources, the local TEC, the Tyne and Wear Development Corporation and so on). Although more recent projections put additional public funding at £73.7m and revised the private contribution downward, it was expected that the claimed leverage of private investment would be greatly increased to £1.2bn, if, as seemed likely, Enterprise Zone status were to be given to a major industrial park within the area.

The local authority provides the partnership with accountancy support, and help with financial monitoring and control and with project development and appraisal.

Partnership in action

Partners, interests, and power

NTCCP includes a wide representation of public, private, voluntary and community interests. Most partners appeared to take the view that there is a good balance of interest representation. It is, however, notable that there was no representation of trade unions on the board. The partnership remained at arm's length from trade union activity such as the recent sustained campaign to save the Swan Hunter Shipyard.

The core of the partnership is between the local authority and private sector interests, built around the activities of City Challenge concerned with regenerating commercial and industrial infrastructure, business support and training. This 'core partnership' builds upon the wider context of public–private partnership to promote the economic development of the North East region. The local authority was widely seen as the dominant force in the running of the partnership. The chief executive came to his post from a senior position in the local authority, and the local authority provided key services to the partnership, as well as substantial additional funding for many projects alongside the City Challenge grant. City Challenge has provided the local authority with substantial direct resourcing of its regeneration objectives, and has allowed it to obtain further funding. The strong commitment of the authority to partnership was linked to a major organisational restructuring, undertaken to enable it to respond more effectively to external challenges and opportunities and the needs of local people. Particular pressures were the council's own declining budget, and the recognition that the authority had become distant from some local communities and was not responding as effectively as it might to social needs, from crime prevention or children's needs to employment.

There is considerable activity by voluntary sector agencies in the area, including a joint facility supported by Barnardos, the church and the local authority on the Meadowell estate. There was voluntary sector involvement in a number of the projects in the action programme, although voluntary sector agencies were aware of other City Challenge partnerships where the sector is more strongly involved.

The partnership also offers substantial representation to community interests. Community representation on the board was considered important to prevent the partnership being a top-down organisation. One partner defined the role of community representatives as "questioning whether projects are truly benefiting the community". Most of the non-community partners considered that a great deal of effort had been put into consulting and involving local community interests, such as those on the Meadowell estate. Community representation and involvement was seen to happen at several levels: through participation in the formal processes of the partnership; through informal contacts with individuals, especially the chief executive and members of his team, who were considered by many partners (including some community representatives) to be open and accessible to local residents; and through the community forums and community development trusts in specific neighbourhoods. There was, though, a widespread view among those interviewed that community involvement in decision-making processes remained rather superficial, although the reasons for this were seen differently. Some partners, especially ones from the local authority, also argued that the local community should be represented through the democratically elected local council, not through 'community' bodies.

Resources, skills and working methods

NTCCP is a multidimensional and multi-partner partnership which is investing substantial resources in a large number of projects. A number of skills and capacities are required for these projects to be realised. These include 'hard' skills of project and programme management and financial control and monitoring as well as the 'soft' skills of partnership working and communication and networking inside and outside the local area.

The local authority was seen to bring to the partnership expertise in planning and land assembly, project control and access to funding, as well as a strategic perspective and representation of the wider community through its councillors. Business partners bring a concern with value for money and commercial viability, and a capacity for risk assessment.

Members of the economic assembly, such as the TEC and the police, also make important contributions. Participation by the police had helped particularly to increase the awareness of some partners, especially private sector partners, of social conditions in areas such as Meadowell.

The partnership draws on the local authority for many of its managerial and technical skill requirements. It appeared to have developed strong systems of programme review and project management and delivery. An important element in these are procedures to allow for flexibility and 'fast track' decisions to be made so that the programme can react to new proposals or circumstances. External consultants carried out an audit for the project's appraisal, monitoring and financial control systems and of tendering procedures. In general, this showed that the systems were functioning efficiently (PIEDA, 1994). The partnership claimed that during the first two years of operation virtually all targets and outputs were achieved or exceeded.

The integrated and multidimensional nature of the programme, and the substantial City Challenge grant, has undoubtedly enabled the project to lever in other public and private investment which might otherwise not have come to the area. Initial estimates of eventual levels of private investment during the five years have since been reduced. This was partly because of the uncertainty over private investment pending a decision about the designation of an Enterprise Zone in the wake of the Swan Hunter Shipyard closure, but also because a major new employer (Siemens), then proposing to locate in the area, would bring into the area a forecast 1,800 new and high quality manufacturing jobs, although of course not all of these would be recruited locally.

In developing effective partnership relationships, informal networking between key individuals was seen by a number of partners to be as important as formal structures and processes. However, some explicit provision was made to promote a common approach, for example, through a one-day seminar for all partners on total quality management (TQM). Some private sector firms have made their training facilities available to the partnership. Training for community organisations is provided by the North Tyneside Voluntary Organisations Development Agency. Regular board meetings are interspersed with topic meetings on key issues, drawing on external expertise.

External monitoring of the outcomes of the programme against an initial social and economic baseline study is undertaken by a local university (Davoudi and Cameron, 1994). The results are discussed annually by the board, and are also considered by the Department of the Environment, Transport and the Regions, which has included North Tyneside in its own national evaluation of the City Challenge programme.

In contrast to the effective networking between public and private sector partners, there was a widespread view that the partnership had not yet drawn effectively enough on the skills and resources of the local community. Some representatives of both public and private sector organisations expressed doubts about the ability of disadvantaged communities to formulate and voice their interests and to manage development projects. While some of the more active community representatives thought that the community forums and development trusts were important in providing a context in which individuals can develop skills and confidence, others were pessimistic about the willingness and/or ability of many residents to take advantage of what they see as opportunities for involvement.

Not surprisingly, local residents often do not find it easy to transcend the daily pressures of coping with poverty and may be unable to relate effectively to the business of the partnership. As one interviewee pointed out:

> "Housewives thrown into a boardroom have difficulty not to feel threatened or to believe that their concerns can override capital development."

Overcoming these problems is more difficult when some partners have limited experience of fostering local involvement. This produced views such as that of one important partner:

> "The community hasn't got many skills so they bring very little to the table. It is here to be consulted, negotiated with, but they [the community representatives] don't help much. They don't speak out much because some of them lack the skills of communication."

Views such as these indicate a gulf within the partnership between many (though not all) partners from public agencies and the private sector, and local residents, a gulf which the system of community representation has been unable to bridge. These views suggest that more time and resources need to be invested in training and cultural change among partners and partner organisations. However, the problem also reflects the emphasis of the partnership on the delivery, within a tight timescale, of a major programme of regeneration projects. The community brings no financial resources to this programme. Community involvement, though desired by most partners, takes second place to the implementation of the programme. Consequently, the partnership has developed efficient systems of management and operation (drawing substantially on the local authority) and effective partnership working among the partner organisations, but has so far had more limited success in involving community representatives as equal partners.

Conflict and consensus

The strategy of the City Challenge partnership was largely determined at the outset by the initial bid for funding. Initially, the proposals were focused strongly on renewal of the economic infrastructure but the 1991 riots on the Meadowell estate brought social issues to the fore. The strategy in the bid combined important elements of economic, social and physical regeneration, providing the basis for a broad consensus among the major partners.

There were, however, differing views about the priority of different elements of the programme. Community and some other partners have criticised the limited expenditure on community projects compared to industrial and commercial projects. An important issue is the distribution of investment between different areas of need, especially the priority which the Meadowell estate has appeared to gain in relation to other similar estates, both inside and outside the City Challenge area. The effect of City Challenge and the associated SRB bid has been to 'ringfence' more than £30m of investment for Meadowell, which might well have been distributed more widely. The partnership responded to this by developing a stronger focus on other areas, especially the other major estate within its area, Howden. Beyond the City Challenge area, however, this issue remained one which the local authority recognised it needed to respond to, requiring a search for other sources of funding to match the City Challenge and SRB investment in other areas.

A different kind of issue had arisen in relation to the closure of the Swan Hunter Shipyard. While the partnership had not been directly involved in the struggle by the trade unions to save the yard, it was strongly aware of the impact of the closure on its targets, especially in terms of employment. It lobbied government to assist the area in the event of closure, arguing that if an Enterprise Zone is to be established in the region, an industrial zone within the City Challenge area should be the main site to benefit from designation.

In general, partners felt that strong and efficient management within the partnership had successfully contained explicit conflict on the partnership board. In contrast, there had been some conflict among local community interests. On the Meadowell estate, the establishment of the Meadowell Forum and Community Development Trust, and the development by the trust of its own strategy for the estate (Meadowell Development Trust, undated), were important steps in building a clear community perspective. However, this proved difficult to sustain, and there were differences of opinion between community workers, representatives and activists which reduced the effectiveness of community representation in the partnership. More experienced community leaders attributed these difficulties to the lack of experience many residents of excluded communities had of community involvement and official procedures, emphasising the need for greater priority to be given to resourcing community involvement, and for extended timescales for local partnership programmes.

Gender and race equality issues

As has already been indicated, there was a major disparity on the board and executive committee between the predominance of (white middle class) males as representatives of public and private sector partners, and of women as community representatives. In the view of one person interviewed, this reflected the macho 'business' ethos of the development industry to which the partnership is primarily orientated, 'with its networking around golf, shooting and business entertainment'. While the partnership offered space for women from communities like Meadowell to participate in the policy process, traditional gender roles had been replicated by the confinement of women to 'community' roles, and the partnership had not really given priority to women's issues in its strategy and activities. While some training for community representatives had been available, most of the (largely female) community partners remained disadvantaged by their lack of familiarity and expertise in the processes of partnership working. Ethnic minorities make up only a very small proportion of the local population and are not represented in the partnership.

Some leading partners did recognise that the partnership now needed to explicitly address the issue of gender representation within the partnership. However, the partnership programme itself, which is unlikely to change in major respects, is organised around issues such as business development, training, housing and infrastructure, not primarily around the needs of social groups such as women (or the unemployed or young people). Even though individual projects may be of value to particular groups, the partnership does not recognise gender and equal opportunity issues systematically throughout its programme.

The impact of the partnership

Partnership as a working method

The major impact of NTCCP is associated with the resources which it has brought to the area, both directly and through leverage. This local demonstration of the rewards of a partnership approach has been reinforced by the more recent success in securing substantial funding from the SRB, the successor programme to City Challenge, and also £5.7m from the national Sports Lottery. The commitment to partnership represents a considerable change from the previous orientation of the local authority. Business interests remarked on the fact that they could 'do business' with the local authority leadership, unlike other 'unreconstructed' local (Labour) politicians still seen as hostile to the private sector.

The partnership has also shown the importance of strong project management when delivering a substantial programme over a short space of time. Its own effective management systems have been important, but so has its ability to draw on the resources of the local authority. Within the local authority, the commitment to the City Challenge partnership has been closely associated with a wider restructuring of the authority's organisation and processes to produce greater internal efficiency and greater external accountability. Here the City Challenge partnership is one of a number of factors which has promoted the development of a broader 'civic leadership' role on the part of local government, alongside its role in delivering services.

City Challenge has been an important force in North Tyneside in establishing the perceived advantages of interagency partnership. A range of stakeholders believe that the inclusion of community representation in the partnership structure has led to a greater understanding by both the private sector and public agencies of problems of poverty and social exclusion. 'The community' was now accepted as a partner in regeneration. As one stakeholder put it:

> "People now have a voice and through the publicity
> process we get them to offer their views on proposals.
> There is a significant difference in the level of
> involvement."

This represented more than the 'official line': some leading figures in the community supported the view that the Meadowell Community Development Trust had made a significant contribution to the empowerment of local people, especially through the election of representatives from different parts of the estate, although others felt that this undermined the democratic role of local councillors and was liable to 'split the community from the Council'.

Impact on social exclusion

Many of the City Challenge partners were very cautious in assessing the impact of the partnership on social exclusion and poverty.

Positively, it was argued that the partnership had improved organisations' understanding of poverty, creating a new proactivity and more joint working. It had involved some members of deprived communities, and provided them with resources for buildings and for business planning, and with new housing, which will be of long-term help.

There was, however, a widely shared view that it was, at best, "too early to say" what the longer term impact of the partnership will be on poverty and exclusion. In the words of one partner:

> "Partnership is working through mutual understanding but it would be foolish to say that poverty is improving yet".

Partners recognised that the City Challenge partnership is "capital not community-led", and that not all the major investment it represents benefits the local community. The 'bricks and mortar' approach to regeneration can transform a small area physically but still have only a limited effect on unemployment, poverty and crime:

> "There has been a limited regeneration in a concentrated geographical area but the central processes – physical infrastructure, private investment – are contradictory."

For example, the Meadowell Community Village on the Meadowell estate is an ambitious project which aims to provide leisure and community facilities at the heart of the estate, and to create jobs and training through the implementation of the development. The first elements of the project, especially the construction of a community centre (replacing facilities destroyed on the 1991 disturbance) were being carried out by a locally formed community construction company with a local social enterprise company. The Community Village was intended to complement the local authority's new 'one-stop-shop' centre which opened in 1993 and an extensive Estate Action programme, and other projects including the creation of a base for the local credit union. However, some partners, especially but not only in the public sector, argued that providing of housing and community facilities is only of marginal relevance if jobs cannot be provided, and that physical regeneration in one place may merely shift poverty to a different neighbourhood:

> "What is required is jobs. Without jobs the rest is Toytown game playing."

Similarly, there was scepticism about the gains from training:

> "Meadowell is a classic example of an area where those who have been able to have gained an education and got out, never to return, and the residue, those left

behind, are unemployable because they are old, infirm, or have lost the work ethic. It is full of people doing nothing and training schemes won't help in such dire circumstances. All competent people get drawn out in such circumstances and we are left with those that can't work and in many cases won't work."

Employment – the primary objective of the City Challenge partnership – was accordingly seen to be the litmus test for the partnership. Until the labour market situation improved significantly, the effect of concentrated high and long-term unemployment in neighbourhoods like Meadowell creates a situation in which the struggle for daily survival dominates the community and negates the potential gains of partnership: "People may have been 'empowered' but the quality of life has not improved."

In its first two years, the partnership claimed to have created 1,019 new jobs and sustained 1,598 more, but, even if these claims can be substantiated, unemployment in the area had continued to rise, and changes in benefit entitlements continued to reduce the disposable incomes of the unemployed. Despite this, as a result of the anticipated Enterprise Zone designation and the arrival of a major employer, the partnership was forecasting that it will significantly exceed its five-year job target and create 3,500 new jobs. The external evaluation being undertaken by the university will be important in shedding more light on progress made on job creation and the extent to which employment is being accessed by excluded groups and communities.

Impact on the wider policy framework

In the UK, the City Challenge programme is widely regarded as an advance on previous regeneration programmes in its advocacy of a broadly based local partnership framework and a broad multi-dimensional approach to regeneration. These features have been continued in the successor programme, the SRB.

NTCCP offers some confirmation that a broadly based partnership can work efficiently, and especially that local government can play a highly effective leading role in local public–private partnership. It provides evidence that the involvement of community interests in local partnership can improve the understanding of problems of poverty and social exclusion within the policy process. But the empowerment of severely excluded groups and communities as equal partners in partnership may be dependent on real progress in tackling unemployment and poverty, and on the ability of local partnership to generate real improvement in the quality of people's lives, as well as on organisational and cultural change in partner organisations.

At the time of the research, the partnership's activity programme was in the middle of its five-year span and so a full assessment is premature. From the beginning it has been recognised that regeneration in North Tyneside and the City Challenge area will require further resources on a long-term basis. The approach of the partnership has been to build a framework within which further resources can be attracted, and this approach was clearly having some success. However, it has also been recognised that local partnerships only have very limited leverage over external economic and political decisions, such as the Swan Hunter closure, which can constantly offset such gains.

Conclusion

The City Challenge programme (with the similar New Life for Urban Scotland programme in Scotland) has been the major UK government urban regeneration programme of the early 1990s, and a major source of government funding for local areas of concentrated deprivation and disadvantage.

City Challenge has encouraged a wider, partnership approach to locally based regeneration than previous schemes. While the intention of government was that City Challenge should be business led, it has offered a greater role than previous government funding programmes to local government and community interests. In North Tyneside, this opportunity has been taken up by the local authority, which has been a leading player in the City Challenge partnership, working closely with business interests and other public and quasi-public agencies. The strong interagency and public–private partnership framework and ideology developed during recent years has created a basis on which further resources for regeneration continue to be attracted, both from the SRB and from EU funds, the national Lottery and the private sector.

In contrast, however, to the rapid progress made in developing public–private partnership, the involvement of excluded communities and social groups in the local partnership framework has so far been much more partial. Despite the formation of community forums and development trusts, active involvement was largely limited to a relatively small number of individuals, and high proportions of the local community showed little knowledge of, or interest in, the partnership.

While women are recognised to play the major role in maintaining the community on estates such as Meadowell, their role in partnership processes tends to reinforce rather than challenge traditional gender roles. Equal opportunity issues are not reflected systematically in the partnership's programme.

In areas of severe deprivation, such as Meadowell and other neighbourhoods, entrenched poverty, and especially unemployment, militates against participation. This emphasises the importance of the City Challenge partnership in creating jobs for local residents, especially for the most excluded groups. NTCCP was achieving some success in this area. However, at the same time, partners recognised that in areas like North Tyneside, while even the scale of resources invested by City Challenge may, at best, make a significant contribution to employment needs, at worst continuing job loss in the local economy may offset any gains made.

The experience of NTCCP shows that in areas of severe deprivation, even strong local partnerships with significant resources remain dependent on external decisions by both government and economic actors.

Chapter 4

The Western Isles and Skye and Lochalsh LEADER Partnership

Background

Context and origins

The Western Isles and Skye and Lochalsh (WISL) LEADER Partnership was funded under the EU's LEADER I (1991-94) programme. The LEADER I local projects were charged with developing innovative, flexible and integrated community-based responses to the development problems and opportunities of rural areas.

The Western Isles and Skye and Lochalsh are situated in the remote North West of the Scottish Highlands and Islands. The Western Isles form a chain of 12 inhabited islands and numerous other smaller ones facing the Atlantic off the western coast of northern Scotland, stretching some 200 km from north to south. The island of Skye and the immediately adjacent Lochalsh area of the west coast mainland lie south and east of the Western Isles. The areas, which are entirely rural, share many natural, economic and social characteristics as a result of their location and history, including the continuing survival of the Gaelic language and culture.

The total population of the area is about 43,500 with more than two thirds concentrated in the Western Isles. Administratively, the Western Isles has been a single-tier local authority, while Skye and Lochalsh was a second-tier district authority within the Highland region. The whole area has suffered a long history of depopulation and out-migration as a result of the marginal nature of the local economy. It has remained largely peripheral to the major processes of urban industrial growth which have transformed other regions, and the most important decisions affecting the local economy have been taken externally. As a result of the very limited development of the private sector, public employment and welfare benefits play a disproportionate role in sustaining local incomes. The principal economic activities of the area are crofting agriculture, forestry, fishing, fish farming and fish processing, construction and quarrying, tourism and the service sector, especially public sector services. The small-scale manufacture of Harris tweed and craft products is important in some areas. Most businesses in the area are small or very small. Only four organisations within the region employ more than 100 people. Self-employment and various combinations of part-time employment are common. Unemployment is consistently higher than in the Highland region as a whole. However, the region is also seen to have a number of potential socio-economic advantages, ranging from the strength of community identity and local culture to the possibilities of tourism and the wider economic potential of the highly attractive environment.

There is a long history of social and economic regeneration and development programmes in the area, dating back to the 19th century. The Highlands and Islands Development Board (HIDB), established in the 1960s, was an innovative regional development agency which supported enterprises in a range of economic sectors, and also operated a social development fund for community development projects. In the early 1990s many of the functions of the HIDB were devolved to a series of LECs, including Western Isles Enterprise (WIE) and Skye and Lochalsh Enterprise (SLE). The establishment of the Western Isles Islands Council (WIIC) as a single-tier local authority in 1975 gave a boost to the social and cultural identity of this part of the area and contributed to a revival of the Gaelic language. The formation in the 1980s of the Scottish Crofters Union gave a stronger voice to the crofting population. EU funding for development has included Integrated Development Programmes in both the Western Isles and Skye.

The direct origin of the partnership lay in a meeting organised jointly by WIE and SLE, to explore the possibility of a LEADER bid. It was agreed that the strong compatibility between the recently prepared development plans of the two organisations, and their similarity to the LEADER aims and objectives, placed the area in a position of comparative advantage. Also, the combined population of the two areas met the threshold for funding (Rennie, 1994). Collaboration with a wider area of the north west mainland was considered but rejected because the area was considered too large and diverse. Support for the proposal was forthcoming from WIIC and Highland Regional Council (HRC), and it was decided to also seek the involvement of two key NGOs, Comunn na Gaidhlig, the Gaelic language development agency, and the Scottish Crofters Union which represents the small farmers of the area.

Partnership structure

The objective of LEADER I was to promote new forms of rural development which would exploit the economic potential of specific local areas but could also serve as models for other areas. The WISL programme was approved in December 1991 (WISL LEADER, 1991). The partnership was formed by the two LECs, WIE and SLE, the two local authorities (WIIC and HRC), Comunn na Gaidhlig and the Scottish Crofters Union. An executive group of 12 members nominated by the six partner agencies was established and met monthly (see Figure 3). The main partners established formal mechanisms for reporting back to their organisations, and these were especially important for the local authorities in enabling local politicians to review progress. In the LECs, the close informal working relationships promoted by location of the LEADER team in the LEC premises were as important as formal reporting procedures.

Local LEADER groups were established to overcome the geographical division and differences in previous approaches to local development between the Western Isles and Skye and Lochalsh. The groups, which met regularly in the two main areas, included the local partner agencies and a number of other important organisations: the Gaelic Further Education College, Sabhal mor Ostaig, local tourism promotion agencies and Scottish Natural Heritage, the government body responsible for natural environment issues.

The executive group took policy decisions, including decisions on major or controversial projects, but the main management and development of the programme was undertaken by a project coordinator and project team. The key post of coordinator was based in the Western Isles, but the partnership also relied on three field officers located in different parts of the area and working with field officers of partner agencies, for the appraisal and development of projects. A network of part-time animators was recruited locally to stimulate project ideas among local people and help work them up into LEADER projects. There was no direct community involvement in the partnership. The project coordinator and two of the three field officers were women, although this was not the result of a deliberate equal opportunities policy. In contrast, nearly all the representatives of partner agencies were men. Reflecting the partnership framework of the programme as a whole, many of the individual projects were funded on a partnership basis by a group of partners and other agencies.

Figure 3: Structure of the Western Isles and Skye and Lochalsh LEADER Partnership

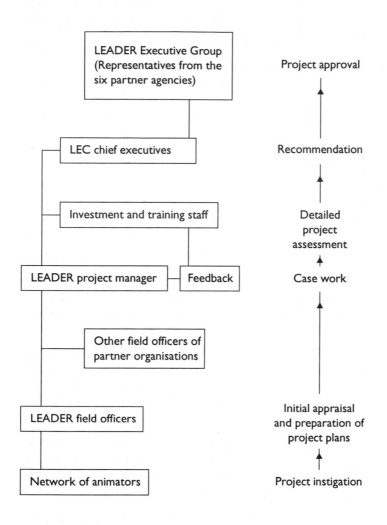

Objectives and activities

The philosophy of LEADER I was that local people are the principal asset of rural areas, and the role of the funding was to help them to identify development opportunities suited to their environment, culture, working traditions and skills. Accordingly, the LEADER programme gave priority to promoting integrated rural development, arranging joint financing of projects, and providing local people with project planning and management skills (Black and Conway, 1995; Arkleton Trust [Research] Ltd and Department of Land Economy, 1994). The information and conclusions contained in the evaluative assessment of the LEADER project by the Arkleton Trust with the Department of Land Economy, University of Aberdeen, has helped to inform the points made in this case study.

LEADER was seen as "'liberating people to think for themselves' by encouraging them to come forward with their own ideas, and assisting them to turn those ideas into action, in contrast to more familiar but constraining packages of set grants for set measures" (Arkleton Trust [Research] Ltd and Department of Land Economy, 1994). The WISL partnership considered investment in local people to be at the heart of its development strategy. The WISL LEADER programme was seen to be a way of moving away from a culture of dependency towards more self-reliant rural entrepreneurship.

Within this broad approach, the LEADER partnership promoted investment under a number of themes, reflecting key sectors of perceived opportunity in the local economy (rather than the needs of particular social groups, such as the unemployed or women or young people):

- support systems for rural development, including the establishment of a network of local animators, a rural development forum, and a network of rural community teleservice centres, and assistance with a natural resources audit for the region;

- vocational training and employment support, including distance-learning materials and courses, establishment of rural training centres and training of instructors, and provision of childcare for women returners;

- rural tourism, including marketing, the promotion and interpretation of key tourist sites, and the development of workplace-based tourism;

- assistance to small firms, crafts and services, ranging from the exploitation of craft produce to new technology-based businesses, and cooperative business premises;

- marketing of the goods, products and attributes of the region, including promotion of the use of the Gaelic language as a marketing tool.

Other measures included support for alternative energy sources, waste recycling and the refurbishment of community buildings. In all, more than 220 projects were implemented.

Funding

The LEADER I programme involved EU expenditure of 450m ecu over the period 1991-94. The WISL LEADER programme received an allocation of £1.4m. Together with national public and private matching funding, it was anticipated that this would lead to a total expenditure of £3.3m. In practice, this figure was easily exceeded, with actual global expenditure of more than £4.9m, due to much higher leverage than anticipated. Funding for the programme was routed via the Scottish Office of the UK government, and the two LECs were designated as the lead delivery organisations for expenditure.

Partnership in action

Partners, interests and power

There was a clear and strong view among all partner organisations that WISL LEADER was generally successful in building a partnership which reflected the interests of the main partners.

The lead agencies were the two LECs, WIE and SLE. The LECs are publicly funded but employer-led agencies responsible for training, business support and enterprise development. The project coordinator was based in WIE (although she also spent considerable time in Skye and Lochalsh) and the field officer for Skye and Lochalsh was based in SLE. While some partners, especially local councillors, thought that this made the project team too close to the dominant partners, it assisted the financial management of the programme because the LECs were responsible for managing the funding. For the two LECs, the LEADER funding enabled them to support projects of an innovative nature which would not have qualified for mainline LEC funding.

The partnership had a major effect in building closer working relations between the two LECs, and between each LEC and the local authorities. One partner contrasted the local partnership approach in the LEADER project with the normal experience of being "hauled into Inverness or Edinburgh" in order for decisions to be made. In the Western Isles, in particular, the LEADER partnership appears to have proved valuable in breaking down distrust between the WIIC and WIE. Factors in this were said to include the willingness of partners to respect each others' views and interests, giving enough time in meetings to 'thrash out disputed issues', and an equitable division of resources between different areas.

The local authority partners had concerns about the lead role of the LECs, which they did not regard as having the legitimacy and accountability of democratically elected local authorities. Nonetheless, there was considerable agreement on the value of the partnership framework in securing LEADER funding, and working relationships among officers at the operational level were generally good. By supporting innovative projects of a social and sometimes more risky nature the LEADER programme was regarded as a valuable supplement to the limited resources of local authorities, and a valuable complement to the business-oriented programmes of the LECs.

The other partners, Comunn na Gaidhlig and the Scottish Crofters Union, played an important role in the development of the programme, especially in relation to its focus on Gaelic culture as an integrating theme linking social, cultural and environmental issues with a grass roots approach to economic development. In practice, the close partnership between the LECs and the local authorities appeared to exclude the other partners in the management and implementation of the programme. However, these agencies still felt that they were able to have an effective say on policy issues if necessary, through steering group and area meetings. There was considerable discussion about the involvement of other agencies (such as Scottish Natural Heritage, for example) which played an important role as project co-funders but were not LEADER partners. Views differed on the possible involvement of more partners when discussing a follow-up LEADER II, but it was felt that the tightness of WISL LEADER I had enabled a strong partnership to be established between the core group of agencies. In this case, some of the success of the partnership is attributed to its small size.

Local community organisations and interests were not directly represented in the WISL partnership, except through the representative role of the local authorities. The partnership attempted to build links to the local community in a number of ways: through extensive publicity; through the work of the field officers; and through the network of local animators drawn from local communities. These are discussed in the following sections.

Resources, skills and working methods

The main partners in the WISL LEADER partnership brought different skills and resources to the partnership. The main contribution of the LECs was in relation to programme and project management and funding. Although not all partners were entirely happy with the close link between LEADER and the LECs, in operational terms it was undoubtedly helpful that there was a close 'LEADER–LEC' partnership which enabled project applications to be processed quickly, and funded projects then managed efficiently. This was particularly important in enabling the programme to achieve funding of a large number of projects despite problems which arose about criteria for project funding, the delayed release of EC funds and the consequent very short timescales for the programme. The LECs were also major contributors of other public matching funding. It is notable that the major spending category was training, closely related to the core activity of the LECs. The contribution of other partners included substantial funding for tourism and economic and social development projects, especially by WIIC. Local authorities and other partners believed that they played important roles in the original formulation of the programme, and in ensuring that, unlike the situation in other Scottish LEADER programmes, the WISL programme remained much broader in its focus than a LEC programme.

Many partners and also recipients of funding considered that the project team played a major role in the success of the WISL LEADER partnership. In particular, the project coordinator was able to establish the autonomy of the LEADER project from the LECs, and cement relationships within the partnership, between the partnership and the local community, and negotiate on behalf of the WISL partnership with the Scottish Office and the European Commission. The decentralised field officers were important in ensuring that the programme operated effectively throughout the very dispersed area, and that effective working was developed between different partners, particularly the LECs and local authorities, but also other partners and contributing agencies, in both the Western Isles and in Skye and Lochalsh.

The system of community animators is a more controversial issue. The animator network is regarded as an important contributor to the

LEADER philosophy of bottom-up development through the stimulation of local initiative. In the absence of direct community representation in the partnership structures, the animators represented an important link between the partnership and local communities. In parts of the area (especially the southern part of the Western Isles) the system worked extremely well in practice, with the animators acting as a highly effective stimulus and channel for local ideas and projects (Arkleton Trust [Research] Ltd and Department of Land Economy, 1994). In other areas, though, it was described as 'a disaster', and field officers appear to have filled the role envisaged for animators. This failure in some areas was attributed to the different capabilities of individual animators but also to the limited training and guidance provided. This was particularly difficult because of the tight timescales within which the programme was forced to operate. Partly because of the pressure of work, full project team meetings took place only every three or four months. It was recognised in retrospect that more training and team building for the project team would have been desirable, for project officers to exchange experience and to give support to the local animators.

The WISL programme was extremely successful in stimulating project proposals, and in securing matching funding. Despite the varying effectiveness of the animator system, funded projects were distributed widely across the area: about half in Lewis and Harris, one third in Skye and Lochalsh and one sixth in the southern part of the Western Isles, a distribution roughly in accordance with population. Overall, funding exceeded the predicted totals in all funding categories especially in tourism projects. This was because matching public funding was more than double the anticipated total; private investment was rather less than projected. The overall ratio of LEADER to matching funding was 1:2.55, with a ratio of 1:1.97 for public and 1:0.58 for private contributions. Of the public matching funding, in addition to the contributions from the LECs and the local authorities, more than £1m was contributed by a range of national and local agencies, from the World Wildlife Fund and the BBC to the local tourist boards and agricultural training boards. This reflects a number of factors: the multidimensional scope and remit of the programme, allowing a wide range of projects, and the efficiency of the programme and project administration, but also the synergy between funders created through interagency partnership. The success of this interagency approach is demonstrated by the fact that the leverage ratio for the WISL LEADER was higher than that for other local LEADER schemes where partnership was less effective (Black and Conway, 1995).

The success of the partnership in generating matching funding means that many of the individual projects were multi-partner projects in funding terms. For example, one of the major projects, the construction of an interpretation centre for the Callanish stone circle in Lewis (a remote area where tourism is difficult to stimulate) involved funding from WIIC, WIE, Scottish Natural Heritage and the Scottish Tourist Board, alongside LEADER money. There was also private sector sponsorship of aspects of the project, such as promotional material.

Conflict and consensus

The broad strategy of the WISL LEADER programme was formulated at the beginning of the programme and formed the basis of the successful bid for funding. The strategy appears to have been sufficiently robust to have provided the basis for implementation of the programme by a range of partners, and flexible enough to allow variation in the uptake of funding under the different categories of development in accordance with proposals made and accepted.

There were differences of opinion as to the type of projects to support – for example, one LEC chief executive argued for more business-type projects – but such issues appear to have been resolved without undue difficulty. In principle, a tension was identified between the LEADER objective of encouraging innovation 'from below', and the development of strategy 'from above', but in practice this does not appear to have been a serious issue because of the scope allowed within the strategy. A more substantial problem appears to have been the difficulty experienced by many applicants in grasping the philosophy of the programme, and recognising that it did not offer tightly specified funding for defined types of expenditure. This problem was intensified by the initial need for members of the project team to establish guidelines for advice to applicants, again compounded by the short timescale of the programme.

The more serious conflicts affecting the programme appear to have been between the local partnership and the UK government and the European Commission. These concern funding mechanisms and the timescale of the programme. At the beginning of the programme, there were uncertainties about the criteria for the funding of projects, and about matching funding. These issues required substantial negotiation with the Commission and with the Scottish Office, which meant that approval for the project was delayed considerably and that the LECs had to provide bridging funding. Flow of funding to projects was consequently delayed which together with the overall limited timescale of the programme put great pressure on the project team in the later stages to process applications. It also meant that some potentially fundable projects were only emerging as the programme terminated. Nonetheless, recipients of funding generally seem to have found the programme accessible and 'user-friendly'.

Gender issues

While women played important roles in the partnership, especially in the project team, this was not the result of deliberate equal opportunity policy, and indeed they were much less well represented in the partnership executive.

The partnership did not take a systematic or proactive approach to identifying or prioritising action for women. The needs of specific social groups, such as women or young people, were only recognised within specific projects, not in the programme as a whole, although some of these projects have brought important local benefits. For example, LEADER funding was the financial catalyst which enabled a local group to establish a day nursery in Portree, the main town on Skye, previously lacking any such provision. The LEADER funding enabled the project to extend provision over the working day to help mothers returning to work, and to develop a childcare training scheme. Projects in tourism created or sustained the number of jobs for women, but not as a result of specific objectives for female employment. However, consideration is now being given to a more directed approach to women's and young people's needs in the LEADER II proposal.

Impact of the partnership

Partnership as a working method

With the exception of the preceding comments concerning the short timescale of the programme, compounded by the initial problems concerning the release of funding, the programme was widely seen in the local area as effective, efficient and innovative.

In particular, the LEADER I programme has been successful in building partnership relations between agencies in the Western Isles and in Skye and Lochalsh, and in stimulating collaboration between the two areas. Partnership has been built both at the level of the programme, and contacts between agencies at the policy level, and through the funding partnerships around specific projects. In the view of one partner:

> "Partnership in LEADER has cascaded through the agencies directly involved, and other agencies are now coming in - Scottish Homes, the Health Board and so on".

The wider impact of the LEADER partnership is confirmed by the external evaluative assessment undertaken for the partnership (Arkleton Trust [Research] Ltd and Department of Land Economy, 1994), which sought the views of leading actors in partner and other agencies and representatives of a range of projects funded by the programme. LEADER is seen to have "shown that partnership can work" both between the two LECs, between the LECs and the local authorities, and among a wider group of agencies. This has been a catalyst for more effective joint working on other issues, at both the policy/political and at the operational level. For example, the establishment of an 'Objective 1 group' in the Western Isles was easier because of the contact through the LEADER partnership.

The success of this partnership has led to the same core partner agencies (with the exception of the Scottish Crofters Union) uniting to submit a LEADER II proposal covering the same area and building closely on the perceived achievements of LEADER I. Partnership is argued to be the core of the LEADER II strategy:

> The local LEADER I programme has demonstrated the potential additional benefit for effective development actions of a **degree of committed partnership**. Partnership through LEADER has come to mean a working together of parties, some with different development agendas, in which all function together for the aims of **integrated development**.... Having laid a foundation for policy based upon collaboration the arena is created in which **innovative methods and solutions** can emerge and flourish; solutions which combine different aspects of development, be it social, cultural or economic. (WISL LEADER Group, 1995)

Impact on social exclusion

Some of the leading agencies in the WISL partnership believed that the problem of social exclusion in the area is associated with peripherality and sparse and declining population as much as with unemployment, income poverty and other factors associated with excluded communities in urban areas (although GDP per capita in the area is only 52% of the UK average). Because exclusion is seen as affecting the whole area, the LEADER scheme made little distinction within the area concerning targeting of specific social groups.

The LEADER programme also did not operate according to specific targets, although forecasts were made of the desirable distribution of investment between the main project categories. The evaluation carried out for the partnership (which was not a requirement of the LEADER programme but was undertaken on local initiative) did not include a quantitative assessment of programme outcomes in terms, for example, of employment created or maintained. Some partners and members of the project team would – with hindsight – have liked more evaluation of some of the main funded projects, and allocation of resources to exploit the successful ones as demonstrations of what could be achieved.

The primary impact of the programme on social exclusion has been to initiate a shift away from the previous 'dependency culture' and 'grant mentality' that has dominated local attitudes to development initiatives in the area, to a more independent and self-thinking attitude. This is the view of the WISL LEADER partners and those associated with LEADER projects referred to in the commissioned evaluation; it has also been confirmed by this research. This shift is closely associated with the nature of the LEADER programme and philosophy, not just the partnership structure through which it was implemented. However, the contribution of partnership was to create a framework in which agencies were willing to reconsider established ways of working, and collectively exploit the new opportunity. While this change in attitude only began to occur towards the end of the programme, the groundwork has been laid to allow future development and community initiative. The partners believe that LEADER II will allow them to reap the benefit of the gains made. Their LEADER II programme proposes to retain much of the approach and partnership structure of LEADER I, although consideration is being given to organising the system of animators on a sectoral basis (for example, horticulture), and to recognise the needs of specific social groups.

The partners consider the major impact the LEADER programme has had on social exclusion is in promoting confidence in communities and in the area as a whole, especially through the strong cultural emphasis of many of the projects. One way in which this was achieved was through support for local historical societies, which play an important role in some communities by recording and keeping alive a historical past which may otherwise be obliterated. The impact of partnership has been in attracting support to projects which would otherwise not have been funded, and attracting a larger than anticipated level of matching funding to its innovative projects. The projects supported extend throughout the area, although it is recognised that there remain major difficulties in stimulating sustainable forms of development in the more marginal communities of the area. Some partners would like to see LEADER II making a sustained attempt to target areas of particular deprivation. It is also recognised that it is too early yet to be clear about the long-term prospects of many of the projects supported. The bid for LEADER II funding is itself a recognition that the problems of the area remain deep seated and that at best the LEADER I programme has demonstrated an approach to rural development which will make better use of future funds than have some of the schemes of the past.

Impact on the wider policy framework

The WISL LEADER project is seen as one of the most successful LEADER projects in the UK and indeed in Europe. It has become a model for rural development in other areas, and in particular for LEADER II proposals. Within the local area, participants in the LEADER partnership welcomed what they saw as the 'unusual independence' offered by LEADER in comparison to other European initiatives, and the potential this gave to agencies to develop locally-tailored policies rather than working to a blueprint imposed from Edinburgh, London or Brussels. This was seen to have widened local aspirations of what European aid could achieve.

However, transference of ideas via the European aspect of the LEADER programme, including ideas about partnership working, was not considered successful because of the limited nature of the exchanges and the difficulties in obtaining resources to organise transnational meetings. While WISL staff did participate in a number of transnational events, distances and travel costs were an obstacle, as again was the timescale restrictions of the programme and the pressure in the later stages due to the early delay in releasing funding. It is unfortunate that there was also a delay in releasing funding at the beginning of LEADER II.

Conclusion

The objective of the LEADER I programme was to find innovative solutions to rural problems suited to the local contexts and relevant to rural areas elsewhere. Within the WISL LEADER, partnership contributed to achieving these objectives in several respects:

- The WISL programme was innovative in establishing a strategy which drew strongly on the social and cultural traditions of the area, and which had considerable success, particularly given the limitations of the timescale, in stimulating bottom-up initiatives.

- The programme seems to have helped to initiate a shift away from a dependency culture to a more proactive and autonomous perspective on the part of local communities. The partnership enabled agencies within the area to work together to develop and begin to apply this strategy.

- The programme has built partnership between a group of agencies which did not previously tend to work together closely, and this has led on to collaboration in a number of further contexts, including LEADER II.

- The programme supported more than 200 local projects spread throughout the local area and many the result of partnership funding. The partnership and its project team and coordinator developed efficient and user friendly systems for allocating funding and in some areas the local animators played a key role as a bridge between the partnership and local communities.

- The partnership contributed and attracted far more matching funding from other public sources than had been anticipated, and also substantial private funding; some of the problems experienced in the early stages of the programme indicate the importance of flexible and rapid delivery of funding to local partnerships from funding programmes.

Chapter 5

Coventry and Warwickshire Partnerships Ltd

Background

Coventry and Warwickshire Partnerships Ltd (CWP) is a locally led economic and social regeneration partnership, bringing together local authorities and other public agencies with local businesses and community and trade union interests. The partnership has attracted substantial government funding from the SRB, the main current UK funding programme for urban regeneration. Within the CWP area, several neighbourhood partnership initiatives in deprived areas, including the Hillfields and Wood End neighbourhoods of Coventry, represent one of the main ways through which the problems of disadvantaged groups and communities are addressed.

Context and origins

Coventry is a major manufacturing city in the English Midlands, whose traditional industries have been a microcosm of the broader West Midlands regional economy based on engineering, especially the car industry. The economy of the surrounding county of Warwickshire is closely linked to that of Coventry both by patterns of travel to work and by interfirm linkages. The West Midland economy boomed in the postwar period as the main national centre of vehicle production when the UK was still the world's second largest producer of motor cars. A high wage economy was built on the prosperity of the region's leading industries and in conditions of close to full employment both skilled and less skilled workers benefited in terms of income and job security. Since the 1970s, however, the dominant picture has been one of de-industrialisation and restructuring of the leading industries and firms, while the growth of new sectors has been relatively limited. The process of economic decline has impacted particularly on certain social groups – women, the unskilled, ethnic minorities and younger and older workers.

The employment base of the local economy is now quite narrow. One in three of the workforce continues to work in manufacturing, where key industries are sensitive to competition and stagnant demand and continue to shed labour. Outside of engineering, there has been significant loss of full-time male jobs as coalmining in the area has been closed down. Although prospects for incoming service sector firms are quite good, the service sector cannot be relied on to replace manufacturing jobs either in quantity or quality. New employment is not, in general, attracted to those areas where unemployment and deprivation are concentrated. These include inner-city neighbourhoods and more peripheral estates.

Hillfields, an inner-city neighbourhood adjacent to Coventry city centre, is one example. This is a multi-ethnic area: of a population of about 9,000, 35% are Asian or African-Caribbean. Unemployment is more than twice that for the whole city, three times the UK figure and more than 50% higher than the EU average. Male youth unemployment and male African-Caribbean unemployment are particularly high. Causes of the high local level of unemployment include job discrimination associated with racism and the stigmatisation of the area, low skill and educational attainment levels as well as poor local employment opportunities. While the majority of housing is publicly owned and in relatively good condition, the private rented sector is poor: one third of households lack central heating and one quarter need substantial repairs. Hillfields has a reputation for crime, and while this is not fully matched by reality there are high levels of racial harassment, drug-related crime and prostitution. The area lacks community facilities and support for the black communities and youth.

Another example is Wood End, a large postwar housing estate on the northern periphery of Coventry. With a population of about 30,000, it is widely considered to be the 'worst area' of Coventry, especially since nationally reported riots in the summer of 1992 led to headlines describing the estate as 'Wood End – Dead End'. The estate suffers the highest levels of vandalism, environmental decay and empty properties, associated with the high density of development, problems with the dwellings themselves, and unsatisfactory estate layout. The area has a high level of unemployment, especially youth unemployment, and high proportions of single parents, children and young people. Only about one in five households own cars and about 70% qualify for housing benefit. There are high levels of burglary and, on some parts of the estate, of drug-related crime. Domestic violence, insecurity and disorder are major problems. Wood End has the lowest average age of death in Coventry and the highest rate of hospital admissions, especially for women and children. Prior to the establishment of CWP, the City Council had pioneered local partnership working in Wood End in a pilot project for area management of public services, although this partnership was limited to public sector agencies (Hayden, 1994).

In Coventry and Warwickshire there is a long history of liaison and ad hoc alliances between public agencies, and between the public and private sectors, in promoting local economic regeneration. For example, the two local authorities collaborated in a joint approach to promoting more environmentally sustainable economic development. The local authorities have also worked with other organisations, including the Chamber of Commerce and the local TEC to bid for UK and European funding. In some deprived neighbourhoods there is a long tradition of community-based organisation and activity, for example, the Community Development Project in Hillfields in the 1970s. This project was followed up in the late 1970s by the Coventry Workshop which built links between local communities, trade unions and the City Council.

However, there have also been local factors inhibiting the development of partnership. The two local authorities have generally been very different in their traditions and political complexions, and in the social and economic issues they face. In Coventry, long-standing Labour control of the Council has traditionally been associated with closeness to the manufacturing trade unions, an arms length relationship with business and a commitment to the Council's own local leadership role and agenda, rather than an active espousal of public–private partnership. However, the urgency of economic and social regeneration, and failure to obtain funding from the City Challenge programme in the early 1990s, proved a spur to the development of a much stronger partnership framework with business and other interests.

An ongoing initiative with major employers to promote the city as a centre of engineering excellence was an example of this. At the same time the City Council, which has traditionally taken a view of a 'unitary city' in policy terms, developed a number of initiatives in deprived areas (such as the area management pilot in Wood End). Their initiatives have offered a more active role to local community interests, and have developed interagency partnership working at local level with the TEC, the health authorities and the police, for example.

Partnership structure

These developments laid the foundations for the creation, in June 1994, of CWP as a formal mechanism for economic and social regeneration through which all organisations concerned with the prosperity of the area could work together and deliver a coordinated programme of action. Initial proposals for a public–private partnership in Coventry itself, strongly promoted by a new director of development in the City Council, were soon extended to include Warwickshire, now under Labour control. This meant that the new partnership covered the same area as the TEC.

CWP claims to be a unique local regeneration partnership in the UK, bringing together public, private, education and voluntary organisations to help build and deliver a coordinated and comprehensive economic strategy for the area. The founding members were Coventry City Council, Warwickshire County Council, the TEC, and Coventry and Warwickshire Chambers of Commerce and Industry. Other organisations joined soon after, including the five second-tier district councils in Warwickshire, the two local universities (Coventry and Warwick) and other higher education institutions, manufacturing and service sector businesses, voluntary and community organisations and trade unions.

The partnership is a company limited by guarantee. Its role is to regenerate the local economy, through developing and implementing an agreed strategy. The partnership operates through a two-tier structure: the 'umbrella' CWP is responsible for the overall strategy, but the intention was that much of the activity of regeneration should be carried out through subsidiary companies and/or partnerships, with their own management structures but responsible to the main partnership for meeting key objectives, as well as by partner organisations themselves. Figure 4 illustrates how its structure works. The first of the subsidiary companies to be formed was responsible for establishing the local Business Link, the new national network of 'one-stop-shops' for business services announced by the government in 1992. Others were being established for tourism development and for the redevelopment of Coventry City Centre.

At the time of this research, the partnership had a board of 25 directors, chaired by the chairman and chief executive of Jaguar Cars. There were seven private sector members, five local government, four from the TEC and Chamber of Commerce, four from higher education, three from the voluntary and community sector (including an ethnic minority organisation) and two from trade unions. The private sector board members were drawn from large and small firms in both the manufacturing and service sectors. Coventry City Council and Warwickshire City Council each supplied two board members, with one from a district council. Many members held their positions in a representative capacity, but for some, especially ones from the private sector, and including the chair, involvement was more personal and individual.

The board has powers to coopt other directors for specific matters. It meets at least four times a year to debate and agree economic strategy, oversee initiatives (for example, the bids for government funding and European grants), to set targets, discuss marketing and promotional activity and to monitor the performance of subsidiary companies.   Working to the board and with responsibility for implementing its decisions is an executive committee of eight members from the four founder partners (Coventry City and Warwickshire County Councils, the TEC and the Chamber).   An officer liaison group acts as a link between the partnership and key partner organisations including local authorities and the TEC.   Formal reporting mechanisms exist to core partners (through local authority committee structures, for example) but are less formal and developed in the case of other partners.   A small project team employed directly by the partnership had recently been established, giving CWP an executive capacity independent of partner organisations.

One of the initial subsidiary partnerships responsible for the regeneration of specific areas and neighbourhoods is the Hillfields Partnership (Coventry City Council, 1994).   This is a community-led partnership, with a core membership (see Figure 5) of residents' groups, voluntary organisations, community organisations, local traders, and two Coventry City Council officers from the development and housing departments.   The local authority provided resources to enable the partnership to develop a 'vision' for the regeneration of the area, as the basis for funding applications to implement regeneration projects.   The core group of the partnership is linked to a community groups network of between 60 and 70 local organisations, which is the main channel into the community itself, and a resource group of senior officers from council departments, the TEC, the police and the health services, which constitutes the link to the activities of local agencies.

Figure 4: Structure of Coventry Warwickshire Partnerships Ltd

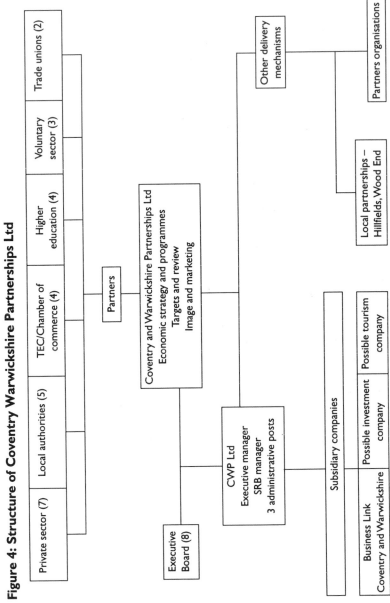

Figure 5: Structure of the Hillfields Partnership

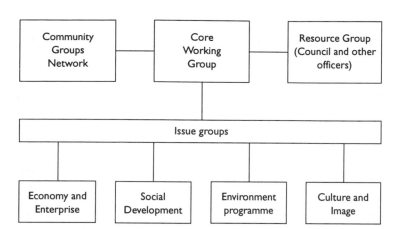

Objectives and activities

The overall aims of CWP are broad. Action to tackle poverty and social exclusion is one element of its wide-ranging economic and social regeneration agenda.

The partnership's strategy was developed by a working party chaired by the vice-chancellor of one of the local universities. The working party assessed the problems and potentials of the local economy and current initiatives being undertaken by partner agencies, and reviewed important changes in the environment for local economic regeneration, such as the role of the new Government Office for the West Midlands, and sources of financial assistance. A draft of the strategy was presented to the AGM of the partnership and it was then published in mid-1995 (Coventry and Warwickshire Partnerships, 1995).

A total of 10 strategic objectives have been identified and grouped within four action programmes concerned with physical regeneration, business development, human and social development, and advocacy on behalf of the area. The objectives of the four programmes are:

Physical regeneration: to promote a high quality and safe physical environment; to strengthen communications; to strengthen the industrial and commercial property base.

Business: to promote the area as a business investment location; to strengthen and diversify local businesses; to support the development of leisure and business tourism; to foster research, development and advanced technology training.

Human and social: to develop workforce skills and enhance employment potential, and to support disadvantaged groups and communities.

Advocacy: to secure funding and support from the UK government and the EU.

The formation of neighbourhood partnerships such as that in Hillfields was seen as an important way to achieve the objective of supporting disadvantaged groups and communities in the human and social programme. In Hillfields, the partnership had developed a 'Hillfields 2000' regeneration strategy, a broad vision of the future of the neighbourhood agreed by the local community, a strategy to achieve the vision, and a series of specific action plans and mechanisms to implement them. The vision was seen as a "forward looking, optimistic picture of how the local community would like their district to develop" (Coventry and Warwickshire Partnerships Ltd, 1995). The vision is of a stronger local community with better community facilities; employment opportunities in line with the rest of the city; a safer and healthier neighbourhood; better shopping, housing and environment; a richer cultural life and a positive image. The strategy to achieve the vision emphasised five sets of measures:

- launching new economic activities;

- improving the prospects of employment for local people;

- improving social, health and security provision;

- improving infrastructures and environmental conditions;

- supporting the improvement of local capacity to solve problems and create partnerships.

Within this, priority was to be given to three social groups: young unemployed people, ethnic minority communities, and people at risk, including single parent families.

The formation of further neighbourhood partnerships was, however, regarded as contingent on local support and the availability of funding to implement locally based initiatives. In some neighbourhoods, such as Camphill in Nuneaton in North Warwickshire, regeneration initiatives are being managed by the local authority in a more traditional manner.

Funding

It is estimated that the partners in CWP were responsible for more than £76m of economic development expenditure in 1994/95. Partner agencies have secured more than £50m in European funds. Much of the area has European Regional Development Fund Objective 2 status and funds have been obtained from RECHAR, KONVER and the European Social Fund.

The major success of the partnership itself has been the securing of £22.5m from the UK government's SRB Challenge Fund for the period 1995/96 to 1999/2000, following a bid for £52m (Coventry and Warwickshire Partnerships Ltd, 1994). Many partners considered that the partnership had enabled them to access SRB funding which would have been difficult if not impossible on an individual basis. The SRB bid was put together by the working party led by the vice-chancellor of one of the universities, which also made the difficult decisions about prioritising projects in the light of available funding. The ability of the universities to play a brokerage role was highly valued by the partnership. The SRB resources allowed the partnership to take a major step towards implementing strategic objectives, through projects ranging from advanced technology and engineering competitiveness to rural transport and social, educational and physical regeneration projects in inner and outer urban areas in different parts of the subregion. At the time of the research, the partnership had prepared a follow-up SRB bid for the 1996 funding allocation, in this instance on a more geographically focused basis.

In relation to Hillfields, a bid was submitted to the EU's URBAN initiative, providing funding for urban regeneration projects, to enable major elements of the local strategy to be implemented, but this was not successful. The new bid to the SRB Fund sought £12.5m in total, including £6m for Hillfields, £1.85m for Keresley, an ex-mining community straddling the Coventry-Warwickshire boundary, and the remainder for a variety of community and economic development projects across Coventry and Warwickshire, for the period 1996/7 to 2000/1.

Partnership in action

Partners, interests and power

CWP brings together a wider than usual range of partners with different interests, converging in the common interest of securing resources for the local area in competition with other localities. The primary interest of the two main local authorities lay in the access which a partnership approach may give to UK government and EU funds for regeneration. For a senior Coventry local politician, regeneration is

> "not something which can be left to the market alone. The local authority knows what it wants to do, and can exercise a leadership role, but needs access to resources and also needs to carry people with it."

For his Warwickshire counterpart, the partnership had greatly strengthened the ability of his authority to obtain substantial funding. A common interest in more effective coordination of policy on a subregional scale was also important, but may have been as much a consequence as a cause of the initial establishment of the partnership. The role of the partnership as a forum for interagency policy making and implementation was perhaps particularly important for the TEC, because of the public–private partnership approach which its remit and activities require.

Among the business partners, some had direct commercial interests in the industrial and commercial development which the partnership may stimulate. Others appeared to have a more indirect interest in ensuring that the policy process promoted the interests of local business, or saw participation in the partnership as a way to fulfil their social responsibilities. Rather similarly, higher education institutions may have a quite direct interest in the funding for training or research which the partnership may secure, but also recognise the more general importance of good local and regional contacts with the policy community.

Some other partners – for example, the representative from the Coventry Racial Equality Council – defined their role more narrowly in terms of representing specific social interests. On the other hand some partners – the trade unions, for example – did not appear to have identified specific interests which they looked to the partnership to realise.

The initial discussions leading to the formation of the partnership envisaged a public–private partnership involving the local authority and private sector interests within Coventry itself, but in a first crucial step this was widened to include the surrounding county of Warwickshire. In this way it came to cover the area of responsibility of the Coventry and Warwickshire TEC and the Coventry and Warwickshire Chamber of Commerce and Industry. Along with the two local authorities these agencies became the four founder partners, and remained the only partners represented on the executive committee.

However, the partnership was then broadened and widened in further ways. Membership was opened to any organisation within the area which accepted the broad aims. At the time of this research the partnership counted 59 corporate members, including the two local universities, other higher education institutions, manufacturing and service sector businesses, voluntary and community organisations and trade unions, and the five second-tier district councils. The board was expanded to reflect the enlarged membership, although many of the members were only involved in the partnership's working processes through their ability to attend an AGM open to all partnership members. The managing director of Jaguar Cars, the largest local manufacturing employer, accepted an invitation to chair the board. There were also six other private sector board members including both manufacturing and service sector and large and small companies. The local authorities had five seats, two each for Coventry and Warwickshire and one for a representative of the district councils. These places were filled by councillors, not officials, and in the case of the County Council there was a deliberate policy to include representatives from both the ruling and opposition parties. (In Coventry the council is dominated by one party.) Some of the districts, however, would have liked to have seen greater representation for themselves on the board.

The TEC and Chamber of Commerce each had two representatives. There were four from the two universities and the higher education institutions, three from the voluntary sector including one from the Coventry Racial Equality Council, and two trade unionists from the Transport and General Workers' Union and the AEU. Community interests were considered to be represented on the board through the local authorities, although there was direct community representation in subsidiary partnerships such as the Hillfields partnership.

As the partnership grew, a number of tensions concerning power and interest representation emerged. An initial fear of some partners – private and public – was that the partnership would be dominated by

Coventry City Council, the largest local authority with a strong economic development staff. The City Council clearly wished to play a leading role in the partnership, and did tend to make the leading resource input to the partnership's activity. The establishment of an independent project team responsible directly to the partnership was important in allaying fears about the council's dominance. Business interests were strongly represented in the partnership structures but some private sector interests still took the view that the expansion of membership has shifted the partnership away from the original vision of a tightly defined economic development partnership. Some private sector members also felt that the partnership has become unwieldy and that this threatened its efficiency. Conversely, some other partners felt that private sector representation needed strengthening through the participation of more leading local firms. They were concerned that the private sector partners did not commit the same level of resources and executive time to the partnership's activities as the main public sector partners, fearing that: "If we're not careful we're going to reproduce the local authority."

The voluntary sector representatives, including the representative of the ethnic communities, made it clear that they would like to see community needs and interests more strongly represented in the partnership. From their point of view, the development of the SRB bid had happened too quickly (admittedly partly as a result of the timescales laid down by government) to allow for adequate consultation and participation.

Given such divergent perspectives, the two-tier structure of board and executive committee was seen as a way to represent a range of interests and ensure effective management. However, several further developments were also seen to be necessary to represent the range of partners' interests more fully. Involvement in the establishment and operation of subsidiary companies/partnerships was presented as a way to involve more members. The role of the new executive manager and project team was regarded as crucial in establishing the autonomy of the partnership from individual partners, and giving it greater capacity to develop and implement its strategy. Some partners considered, however, that the project team was small in relation to its potential workload. Those involved recognised that the partnership needed to communicate more effectively with the range of interests and communities throughout the area. As a first step, a partnership newsletter was being produced to keep members and partner agencies informed.

Resources, skills and working methods

There are essentially two types of resources available to the partnership: those (either in cash or kind) contributed by partners, and resources obtained by the partnership from external sources, especially from UK government and EU programmes.

In its initial stage, up to the successful attraction of SRB funding, the partnership had to draw exclusively on the resources of its members to develop a strategy and apply for the SRB Challenge Fund. While both private and public sector partners were involved in both processes at board and steering committee level, the main commitment of resources was by public sector agencies, especially Coventry City Council and Warwickshire County Council and the (quasi-public) TEC. The two universities also contributed substantially by chairing the two working parties responsible for the development of strategy and for the SRB bid. Since then, SRB resources have been used to help establish the partnership team (alongside contributions from the two local authorities and the TEC). However, the main administrative and operational resource demands of the partnership continue to be met by the leading public sector partners, with only limited inputs of either money or personnel from the private sector (or the voluntary sectors and the trade unions, although of course the resources of the latter two are more limited).

Adapting to the partnership framework has raised substantial issues for both officers and politicians in the local authorities. In Coventry, the commitment to the partnership reflected the view of the Labour leadership that while the City Council should lead the regeneration process, it needed the resources to do so and needed to carry the community (and the business community) with it. For officers, partnership has required important changes in ways of working. This has included the restructuring of the Council's economic development activities, involving a change of employer to the partnership for some employees, or to a subsidiary company such as that running the Business Link scheme. In Warwickshire, the partnership has meant new levels of collaboration with Coventry City Council and with the district councils, and secondments to the Business Link subsidiary. For the district councils it has meant an opportunity to become much more involved in economic development than in the past.

The successful SRB bid resourced the partnership to undertake a range of projects over a period of five years. This is despite the fact that the resources obtained were only half of those bid for, and even if much of the money is recycled from previous grant schemes rather than 'new' money. Lead (including financial) responsibility for each of the funded projects was devolved to one of a small group of core partners (Coventry City Council, the TEC, four of the district councils, the two universities and the West Midlands probation service). Coventry City Council took responsibility for 33 out of 52 projects accounting for well over half of the £22.5m funding. Most of the projects themselves involved a multi-partner contribution. Implementing the full portfolio of projects, involving a range of local project partners and the group of lead partners, was a major management challenge for the partnership. Within the project team, an SRB manager had the important responsibility of overseeing and directing the progress of the programme as a whole and liaising with the regional Government Office. At the same time, the partnership was continuing to seek to attract further resources, both from the next 'round' of the SRB and from European programmes and initiatives.

Conflict and consensus

CWP had still only been in existence for a short period at the time of this research, but during that time it had succeeded in developing a broad strategy on a consensual basis, and this had provided the context for the successful attraction of substantial funding.

In building consensus, the partnership had to grapple with the different interests of partners, and with the different cultures of the various categories of partner. The process of managing and overcoming differences of interest was tackled through two parallel processes: developing a strategy, and developing the SRB bid and the subsequent allocation of funding. Both of these processes were explicitly recognised as opportunities to reflect different interests and to start to forge consensus. A working party chaired by the vice-chancellor of Coventry University was responsible for developing the strategy. Despite the short timescale necessitated by the deadlines imposed by the SRB, it proved possible to undertake a wide, although inevitably limited, consultation with about 400 organisations in preparing a strategy document which was broadly endorsed at the partnership's AGM. It was recognised, though, that it had not at that point fully taken into account the views of some partners, including voluntary sector organisations, ethnic communities and the district councils.

On the other hand, some of the founding business interests felt that the strategy had become too wide ranging and the original business focus was in danger of being diluted. These were seen as concerns to be addressed as the partnership moved to translate the strategy into a business plan in the next phase of activity.

The successful first SRB bid and allocation was similarly undertaken by a working party under the leadership of the vice-chancellor of Warwick University. The truncated timescale was again a problem, and it was necessary to make difficult choices among competing projects both in formulating the bid and in allocating the resources offered, which were only sufficient to finance half the bid. Nonetheless, the final allocation appeared to offer something to a wide range of interests and to have avoided major conflict.

The partnership had also encountered differences of organisational culture, reflected in different assumptions about how it should be run. The perspective of key private sector partners was that boards and executive committees make decisions, which managers then implement. Small, tight decision-making structures were favoured. In the view of public sector partners, managing bodies need to have a greater concern with interest representation and debate: the partnership is a not-for-profit business and therefore its board is bound to have a representational as well as a decision-making role. From both perspectives, the roles and membership of the board and executive committee were thought to need some review.

CWP had thus to address differences of interest and culture between public and private sector partners, between public sector agencies, and between the 'core' partners and others. Not all of these have been overcome: one characterisation of the partnership was that it is "working, but with a constant sense of tension". However, almost all types of partner seemed to share the general view that it has achieved a considerable amount in a short while. In the words of one leading individual:

> "... it must work: the alternative is sectarianism and polarisation. At least if you can have a debate you have a chance for rational forces to come to bear".

Gender and race equality issues

There was no formal provision for the representation of women in the main partnership and only three of the 25 board members were women. There were three individuals from ethnic minorities. The growth of membership of the partnership had been an organic process starting with a core group of white male individuals and, in the absence of specific initiative to promote equality and nominate women and ethnic minorities to the partnership, this had produced a position in which white men play the leading roles.

In general, gender and race equality issues had a low profile in the partnership's strategy and working practice. While this is probably consistent with existing practice in some member agencies and organisations, others, such as Coventry City Council, had developed active policies in this area, and there appeared to be a danger that the transition to partnership may mean a loss of good practice unless stronger action is taken. Local partnership structures, such as those in Hillfields and Wood End, tended to have much stronger representation of women and ethnic minorities and a more proactive stance on equal opportunities issues, suggesting important lessons for the main partnership.

Impact of the partnership

Partnership as a working method

Support for partnership as a preferred way of working is stronger for some partners than others. In CWP, the TEC, for example, needs a strong private–public framework to be effective in delivering training, and is required by its contract with government to work in partnership. For other agencies, both public and private, partnership may only be a preferred working method if it delivers outcomes that are otherwise unavailable. In this respect, CWP had a major impact because it delivered substantial resources through the successful SRB bid. Consequently, partnership was seen as a preferred working method not because it is efficient per se (indeed, there was considerable awareness of some of its inefficiencies and costs) but because it had levered in resources otherwise unlikely to be available. This was particularly the case for all the local authority partners.

For the private sector, the perceived advantages of partnership appeared to lie in the opportunity for a direct private sector voice in the local policy arena, because "politicians don't represent the full spectrum [of opinion]". Partnership is seen as a way to get the public sector to "talk the language of business". For other partners in Coventry and Warwickshire, in particular the voluntary and community sectors and the trade unions, the value of the subregional umbrella partnership still appeared to be a more open issue dependent on their fuller involvement.

There was, not surprisingly, a shared view that it was too early to properly judge the impact of the partnership, being only a couple of years into its operation. In particular, the tight timescales imposed by the SRB deadlines had made it necessary for the partnership to prioritise key objectives – the strategy, the SRB bid – over working processes. At the time of this research no formal evaluation of the partnership's effectiveness had been carried out, but the board was considering how to remedy this. It planned to monitor and evaluate both the SRB projects (through monthly returns and quarterly reports to the partnership) and the progress of the partnership in implementing its overall strategy, including the process of partnership working itself.

Impact on social exclusion

CWP is a broad and multidimensional regeneration partnership. It covers a large area, from the wealthy and prosperous to the deprived, poor and excluded. It has a wide multidimensional remit, including physical regeneration and investment, business development, as well as social and human development. The partnership intended to work through subsidiary companies and partnerships (which can be both issue and area-based), and through projects managed by partners and involving specific sets of local partners. The issue of the impact of the partnership on social exclusion is a complex one, particularly as it was still early in the life of the partnership and the SRB projects were only just getting off the ground. Nonetheless, CWP raises important issues concerning the effectiveness of the SRB (the main current source of UK government funding for local regeneration), the relation between initiatives in poor neighbourhoods and wider city or city-regionwide strategies, and between economic, physical and social dimensions of regeneration in tackling poverty and social exclusion.

The strategy developed by CWP reflected the dominant view in the partnership that regeneration must be broadly based and socio-economic in focus. Economic growth was seen to be the indispensable condition of local regeneration, which then needed to be targeted to the areas and social groups in need. The partnership framework was intended to assist disadvantaged groups in several ways:

- through the funding secured from the SRB, which will benefit deprived areas which would have been unlikely to have attracted such funding otherwise, such as the Camphill estate in Nuneaton in North Warwickshire; other SRB projects are also located in other deprived areas, including Wood End in Coventry, and support youth and ethnic community projects;

- by coordinating action between agencies, for example, to establish credit unions in deprived areas, training schemes for disadvantaged groups;

- by joint action to overcome barriers to employment, including joint initiatives between public agencies and employers to prevent discrimination, to provide access to childcare and training opportunities, support for voluntary sector agencies, and improve transport for rural communities.

Within the subregional partnership framework, local partnerships, such as that in Hillfields were intended to ensure that particularly disadvantaged neighbourhoods could develop their own local strategies and gain benefits from the wider initiatives of the partnership, given that the scale of the subregional partnership, and the current balance of partner representation is not conducive to direct involvement in the umbrella partnership. The Hillfields partnership was regarded as a framework within which local people and groups could agree a regeneration strategy, and as a means to attract resources which the city council could not provide on its own. Although the URBAN bid was unsuccessful, the second round SRB bid made in 1995 was targeted on Hillfields.

However, the targeting of certain areas and groups in a context of resource constraint implies an absence of resources for others. A major cause of concern for the partnership was the limited resources available in relation to need. For one partner, who had been particularly involved with the SRB, it is "a worrying structure, which sweeps up previous programmes and then cuts the money". There was concern that the SRB funding was creating a 'twin-track' programme, with a dominant stream of advanced training and research and development investment to promote economic competitiveness, and a secondary stream of social projects for disadvantaged groups and areas, with inadequate linkage between the two.

In terms of its impact on social exclusion, the partnership was at an early stage. It had targeted some of the most seriously deprived areas and excluded groups, and obtained funding for a range of relevant projects. Further substantial funding continued to be needed, however, both in these areas and in others which have not yet received priority, so that a more integrated approach to implementing the broader strategy could be developed. This would then ensure that the partnership did not differentiate between support for the advanced and competitive element of the regional economy, and social projects in the poorer areas.

Conclusion

Although it is still in its early stages, CWP is likely to be monitored with interest in the UK as one of the leading examples of local partnership associated with the new SRB. As such, it illustrates the extent to which the local partnership approach to regeneration is penetrating the policy community, driven by the requirements of UK government and EU funding programmes. Strong local partnership is now a necessity for localities to compete with other areas for limited regeneration resources. CWP exhibits a number of specific features:

- Partnership working is embedded in a formal framework, with legal status, which is independent of specific sources of funding.

- There is a wide range of partners. Although the private sector is numerically dominant in the main partnership body, in practical terms the public sector remains at the heart of the partnership. In particular, the partnership framework brings together two very different local authorities, together with second-tier authorities, to undertake economic regeneration at the subregional level. Trade union and voluntary sector interests are represented, but are not at the core of the partnership.

- The two-tier structure of an umbrella partnership with subsidiary partnership companies operating in relation to specific issues and in specific areas is seen both as a way to grapple with a range of issues and involve many partners.

- The partnership has a wide remit, ranging from business development and industrial competitiveness to the problems of deprivation and social exclusion in specific areas, and the promotion of socially and environmentally sustainable growth. This does, however, raise important issues about the priority given to problems of poverty and social exclusion within a wide regeneration strategy.

Part Three: Conclusions

Chapter 6

Conclusions and recommendations

This research offers a number of conclusions and implications for the future of the local partnership approach to problems of poverty and social exclusion. This chapter draws together the main issues for partnership at the local level in the UK, reflecting particularly on the conclusions of the three case studies but also referring to experience in other localities where this is relevant. It puts forward a number of recommendations for more effective local partnership. It then considers the implications and makes policy recommendations for different partners, for national policies and programmes in the UK, and for EU policies and programmes. Finally, it makes recommendations for future policy.

Towards more effective local partnership responses to social exclusion in the UK

The concept and practice of local partnership as a framework for tackling poverty and social exclusion and promoting local regeneration has acquired widespread legitimacy in recent years. Broadly based local partnerships involving public, private and voluntary sectors and local community interests are widely seen to be the way to ensure that local strategies and initiatives have broad support, and to provide the basis for a multidimensional approach to the regeneration of local areas, enabling problems of poverty and social exclusion to be addressed alongside those of economic revitalisation and physical renewal. In some places, but not everywhere and to the same degree, this appears to be proving fertile ground for policy integration, innovation and enhanced effectiveness. Where they are successful, partnerships may create new arenas at a local level in which alliances can be built to address the pressing problems of deprivation.

Local partners: a ladder of involvement?

The most direct impetus behind the growth of local partnership has been the fact that increasingly both UK government and EU funding programmes have required a strong partnership framework as a precondition for access to funding, not merely for the implementation of local schemes. Beyond this partnership can bring a number of advantages for policy makers. By identifying a common agenda and strategy, and achieving the commitment of mutual resources, partnership promises to promote synergy and provide a means to manage conflicts between players. The ability of partnerships to manage conflicts successfully is a central question for the partnership approach to problems of poverty and exclusion, where power and resources need to be diffused towards less favoured areas and social groups, and where a convergence of interests between all partners cannot be assumed.

The local partnerships described in this research show that important aspects of broadly based partnership involving public, private and voluntary and community sectors can work effectively. However, the research also shows that not all partner categories are represented equally effectively. Something of a 'ladder of partnership involvement and influence' often exists. The greatest involvement – including a leadership role not confined to the representation of specific interests – is generally that of local government and sometimes of other local public or semi-public agencies, especially the TECs (LECs in Scotland). Other public agencies – health authorities or the police, for example – may be actively involved but with a more specific focus on their core areas of responsibility. Employers and employer organisations are often strongly represented on partnership structures (including through TECs or LECs), but the extent of their commitment is often limited to a narrow conception of their direct economic interests rather than a wider partnership agenda. Voluntary sector agencies are normally represented and make important contributions including involvement in specific projects within activity programmes. Community organisations and representatives are normally (but not universally) represented on partnership bodies but not as equal partners. Trade unions are only represented on some occasions and do not generally play a major role.

Recommendations

• Local partnerships should be broadly based to ensure effective representation and involvement of public, private, voluntary and community interests.

• Partnerships should particularly ensure that voluntary, community and trade union interests have the opportunity to be effectively represented in core partnership bodies.

Further implications for different partners are discussed below.

Partnership structures

The involvement of a broad range of partners in local partnerships brings both gains, in terms of interest representation, and challenges, in terms of efficient organisation. However, partners often continue to have different views about effective management styles and structures, so it would be useful to identify the advantages and disadvantages of different approaches and models. Two solutions are frequently adopted in this respect. A two-tier structure of partnership organisation is often adopted (a board and an executive) especially in the larger partnerships. This sometimes reflects an implicit distinction between representation and management functions. In some partnerships, such as the Western Isles and Skye and Lochalsh LEADER Partnership, a deliberate decision was taken to keep the partnership management body small, and this may be a useful approach where the area covered by the partnership is restricted. Even in this case, however, the decision to retain a 'tight' core partnership excluded some organisations and also direct local community representation.

The way in which individuals are nominated or elected to positions in local partnerships is an important question in the UK because of current concern with the erosion of local democracy by the increasing number of non-elected appointments to state or quasi-state bodies or quangos. In most local partnerships, most members are nominated by their organisations or constituencies, often because of their personal interest and commitment (although in local authorities, for example, individual nomination may need to be confirmed by the Council). Some community representatives are elected from neighbourhood bodies. In most cases, the nomination is either for the duration of the partnership programme, or for an unspecified period. Reporting arrangements between individual representatives and their organisations vary considerably from clear and explicit procedures established by some partners to much less formal and limited ones. While most members of partnerships are likely to continue to be appointed or nominated rather than elected, it is important that these processes are as effective, accountable and transparent as possible. This need not dilute the ability of partnerships to attract individuals with the requisite expertise and commitment.

In most partnerships, considerable responsibility for strategy implementation is devolved to a partnership or project team. The skills of this team can have an important impact on the success of the

partnership.   These include: skills of networking, both between
organisations and in the community; programme and project
development, management and evaluation; fundraising and financial
management.   In some cases, the small size of the project team
established by the partnership means that only some of these skills are
represented.   Resources – of both time and money – will be necessary to
develop the skills of the project team.

Recommendations

- A two-tier partnership structure is often helpful in combining
efficient operation with the representation of different partners'
interests, although this may need to avoid the development of a
privileged inner group of partners.

- Mechanisms for nominating or electing representatives to partnership bodies, and for reporting back to their organisations or
constituencies may need to be reviewed to ensure that individuals
represent the interests of their constituencies effectively.

- Partnership project teams need to have, or have access to, a
considerable range of skills, and resources for skill development.

Gender and race equality issues

In many partnerships (including the case studies discussed here), the
representatives of community and voluntary sector partners are often
women. The majority of members of some project teams are also
women. It is much less common for women to represent other partner
interests, and to occupy powerful positions on partnership management
boards. While it is increasingly recognised that women play a crucial
role in maintaining some sense of community in deprived
neighbourhoods (Campbell, 1992), this experience is often not
available at the heart of partnership processes. In areas where ethnic
groups are important in the local population and suffer particular
problems of poverty and exclusion, they may well not be strongly
represented within partnership structures. Key funding programmes
such as City Challenge and the SRB have included few structural
safeguards on representation. Partly because of this, some partnerships
exhibit a passive rather than a proactive attitude to gender and race
equality issues, although there are notable exceptions to this, such as the
Brownlow Community Trust or the Granby-Toxteth Community
Project.

Recommendations

- Local partnerships need to consider specific mechanisms to involve, and reflect the interests of, women and of ethnic minorities. These might include: targets for gender and minority representation on partner bodies; addressing barriers to full participation by women and ethnic groups (language, childcare, times, places and formats of meetings and so on); consultative forums for women and ethnic interests.

- Local partnerships can draw on examples of good practice such as those offered by some of the partnerships discussed in this research.

- Where good practice exists within partner organisations, partnerships should ensure that they adopt this as well.

Objectives and remits

In the UK the remit of many local partnerships is wide, including strategy and programme development, project generation and management, as well as coordination, catalysing and advocacy activity. Many local partnerships are multidimensional, not just in the sense that they involve a multi-agency and multisectoral approach to poverty and social exclusion, but in the sense that they often include local anti-poverty action within a broader local regeneration agenda. This includes the physical regeneration of deprived neighbourhoods and the promotion of local economic competitiveness as well as a concern with deprivation and exclusion. The specific focus of the Poverty 3 projects on poverty and exclusion has been a notable exception to this, but practice and thinking in the UK has tended to be dominated by the larger national government programmes, City Challenge and the SRB.

Some of the advantages and disadvantages of this approach are evident from the case studies. The 'comprehensive local regeneration' approach potentially allows problems of poverty and poor areas to be tackled within a broader and more inclusive framework, and by initiatives drawing on substantial public and private investment. The danger, however, is that problems of poverty and exclusion will not be effectively prioritised within strategies and activity programmes. A particular concern is the priority given by local partnerships to job creation, and the limited extent to which new employment is accessed by excluded groups. These issues relate not only to the priorities embodied in national funding programmes, but also to the makeup of local partnerships and where the power lies within them.

Recommendations

- The ability of local partnerships to tackle the multidimensional nature of problems of poverty and exclusion in a concerted way is one of the principal advantages of a partnership approach.

- Where national programmes and local partnerships have remits which extend beyond a concern with poverty and exclusion (for example, to local economic competitiveness) objectives concerned with poverty and exclusion must not be subordinated.

Resources

Most local partnerships in the UK are heavily dependent on resources from national government or European funding programmes. The more successful ones have utilised these resources to lever in further public funds and also private investment.

Local partnerships, and stakeholders in them, are now increasingly recognising the need for a framework which can generate a continuing flow of funding to sustain partnership strategies over more than a four- or five-year period. This reflects not only greater awareness of the deep-seated nature of poverty and exclusion in some deprived areas, but also that local economic regeneration is not just a matter of a once and for all renewal of the local economic base by a short-term project, but necessitates ongoing adjustment to constant economic change.

There are few examples of developed partnership which are not able to rely on government or EU funding. It is therefore difficult to see how the benefits of the local partnership approach can be extended to many of the other areas of need, unless more resources are available from UK government and EU programmes. This would, in turn, enable more matching funding, both private and public, to be levered in to help tackle poverty and exclusion.

Recommendations

- Local partnerships concerned with poverty and exclusion need access to long-term funding; short-term funding is likely to be an inefficient use of resources.

- More resources will be needed if the benefits of the local partnership approach to social exclusion, especially its capacity to lever in additional resources, are to be adopted more widely.

Benefits and costs

A major gain of partnership for any specific locality is often an enhanced ability to attract funding in competition with other localities. This is achieved in a national policy context in which competition for resources is becoming increasingly generalised (as opposed to bureaucratic allocation of resources on the basis of a hierarchy of needs determined by experts, or through more traditional political lobbying). The current UK model of local partnership may be defined more precisely as intralocal collaboration for interlocal competition. The danger of this is that it does not necessarily imply a more general policy gain through partnership, unless it can be shown that this approach leads to a more effective overall use of resources. This may potentially happen in two ways: as a result of either the collaborative or the competitive element of the system. Local collaboration may result in policy coordination, synergy, and policy innovation; the pressure of competition may stimulate these effects.

The case studies indicate examples of these possibilities. In all three areas, successful competition for funding from both UK government and EU programmes has brought in new resources. The creation of local partnerships has also brought further gains through interagency collaboration at the local level. In Coventry and Warwickshire, the partnership has enabled regeneration to be tackled on a scale reflecting the reality of local economic and labour market relationships. In the Western Isles and Skye and Lochalsh, partnership has produced policy innovation both within agencies and from grassroots initiative. A strong strategic partnership framework can generate synergy in funding specific projects.

It is, however, difficult to make a systematic assessment of such gains of partnership working. Indicators of financial leverage are valuable but leverage can be attributed to the characteristics of funding programmes as well as to partnership.

In a more limited sense, there is evidence that partners recognise the value of a partnership approach in sharing the risks and responsibility of managing difficult or intractable policy problems.

If these are the gains what are the costs? Stakeholders in the partnerships discussed were very aware of what can be called the transaction costs of partnership. As one commented: "Partnership takes time, needs money and management".

In both North Tyneside and Coventry and Warwickshire, there was concern about the demands partnership made on all main partners –

public sector agencies, the private sector, and voluntary sector and community partners. These demands impact on senior as well as more junior personnel. Members commented that partnership funding seldom fully reflected the management and other costs of partnership working. The implication is that these costs need to be more fully recognised and budgeted for in programmes, if partners are to be able to maintain their levels of commitment.

Recommendations

- If the local partnership approach is to do more than reallocate scarce resources between localities, local partnerships and funding programmes must identify and monitor the additional benefits of partnership working compared to other methods of developing and implementing policy.

- Programmes and local partnerships must allocate adequate resources to meet the demands of partnership working.

Making local partnership work

Effective partnership needs to work at both the strategic or policy level, and at the operational or project level. This needs both 'hard' and 'soft' skills, ranging from programme management and financial control to vision, and skills in communication and interpersonal relations. The former are sometimes underestimated, but the local partnerships discussed in this research show the importance of efficient programme and project management. In the LEADER partnership, for example, the constricted timescales meant that efficient processing of applications for assistance was crucial to the success of the programme. There is evidence that partnerships can be helped by relying on a leading partner, for example for management and financial skills, as long as this does not imbalance relationships within the partnership. The presence within partnerships of players able to play a brokerage role is also valuable. The important contribution of project teams – and individuals with a range of skills – has already been emphasised.

There is much discussion in the literature and among practitioners of the 'soft' skills of 'partnershipping', such as networking and communication skills, especially the need to employ the different skills and experience of partners. There is less evidence of a systematic approach to identifying the different contributions and perspectives of the public, private and voluntary sectors, and how to make best use of these within a local partnership. In particular, attention should be given to blending a concern for efficiency, clarity of goals and objectives and the need to succeed within given constraints, with the construction and maintenance of a broad consensus and commitment among partners to a common strategy. Local partnerships will often find it worthwhile to devote resources and develop explicit processes for blending organisational cultures and partner contributions within partnership management bodies.

Recommendations

- To achieve effectiveness, local partnerships need to be able to deploy both 'hard' and 'soft' skills.

- In some instances, partnerships may want to call heavily on the skills and resources of a leading partner, but care must be taken to ensure that this does not lead to an imbalance of power within the partnership.

- Partnerships may need to develop mechanisms and processes to identify and blend the different cultures and contributions of different partners.

Partnership with excluded communities

A crucial issue for the effectiveness of partnerships in tackling poverty and social exclusion is the limited degree to which many local partnerships appear to be making 'partnership with the community' a reality. The three case studies in this research demonstrated several approaches to community involvement and empowerment:

- community representation on main partnership boards (North Tyneside);

- community representation in neighbourhood partnerships and forums (for example, in Hillfields in Coventry, Meadowell in Tyneside);

- local 'animators' as a channel between local communities and the partnership (Western Isles and Skye and Lochalsh LEADER);

- openness and accessibility of leading individuals in partnerships to local people.

However, all of these mechanisms appear to have achieved only limited results, especially in involving and empowering the most excluded groups and communities. Many local partnerships have attempted to develop a bottom-up element of community participation, but often both public and private organisations are unable or unwilling to let go of the necessary degree of power and control. They often have limited awareness of what community involvement really involves, and have few policies to support it.

The involvement of women, and the reflection of women's perspectives in local partnerships is a major case in point of the wider issue of involving local communities and excluded groups. It is widely recognised that women's patterns of life give them direct experience of the issues confronting local partnerships. Women's activity has been described as "the glue holding our cities together" (Kitchin et al, 1994), and this is especially true in many of the deprived and excluded neighbourhoods. The specific issues confronting women, and the specific contributions they can make to combating social exclusion, need to be recognised in local strategies and action to identify both problems and solutions. The reflection of women's perspectives in policy needs to be established across the board, not just in a separate 'women's agenda'. Similar action is necessary if the needs of ethnic minorities are not to be marginalised in 'colour blind' partnership programmes. In the first round of SRB funding, there were no ethnic minority-led successful bids, and very few which prioritised ethnic minority issues (Chelliah, 1995).

Some of the ways in which these issues can be taken into account is indicated by examples of local partnerships discussed earlier. Projects such as those in Wood End, Granby-Toxteth and Brownlow show that it is possible for local partnerships to make use of the immediate and direct involvement which women and ethnic minorities have of poverty and exclusion within local communities. The Brownlow Community Trust developed a strategy which focused on the needs of women as one of three priority groups and developed numerous projects for and with women. This activity is being continued by the trust under new funding following the end of the Poverty 3 programme. In Wood End in Coventry, initiatives taken to promote local management of local authority and other public services also explicitly prioritise women's issues, for example, through a concern with domestic violence as well as the more well publicised public disorder issues in Wood End. The Granby-Toxteth Community Project sought (though less successfully) to prioritise the needs of ethnic minorities.

Recommendations

- Local partnerships often need to take more measures, extend their activities, and examine their own procedures and cultures and those of partners critically, if they are to make a reality of partnership with the community, especially with the most deprived and isolated social groups (Chanan, 1992).

- Equal opportunity issues must be given more priority in local strategies. Local partnerships need to recognise the equality dimensions of the various elements in multidimensional local strategies, from employment and training to housing and transport, community safety and health.

- Specific resource allocations may need to be made to meet these objectives, along with provision for monitoring the outcomes of policies and project.

- Stronger guidance on these issues is desirable within mainstream UK funding programmes such as the SRB, and European programmes.

Wider impact of local partnerships

The more successful local partnerships provide evidence of the way in which the benefits of partnership working may become more generalised. The success of the Western Isles and Skye and Lochalsh LEADER partnership, for example, has promoted stronger local partnership relations among a widening group of agencies as well as changing attitudes within partner organisations. This partnership has also been seen as a model for other areas seeking LEADER II funding. In North Tyneside, local and regional public–private partnerships are seen to complement and reinforce each other. In Coventry and Warwickshire, the partnership started from a narrow base but attracted much wider involvement.

In some partnerships, however, there is a need to increase involvement among the local business community, especially major employers in the local economy.

The experience of the LEADER programme, among others, also suggests that more resources may need to be allocated to facilitate the exchange of good practice, including greater emphasis on evaluating and disseminating examples of successful partnership working. Learning needs to take place within specific partnership-based programmes but also between different programmes including both government and EU-funded programmes, and both within the UK and transnationally.

Recommendations

- Greater emphasis needs to be given to disseminating the gains from partnership, within and among national and European programmes.

- At a local level, there may be a need for partnerships to extend their impact in the business community beyond the participation of a limited number of employers and employer organisations.

Partnership and social exclusion

The local partnership approach may contribute to combating poverty and social exclusion in two linked ways: by bringing resources and investment which materially improve the quality of life of excluded groups and communities, and by empowering the excluded to improve their own situation.

The research suggests that in some places – North Tyneside and Castlemilk, for example – local partnerships have improved the understanding of problems of poverty and exclusion among both public and private partners, and have contributed to a more integrated policy approach. At the same time, those involved in local partnerships are often acutely aware of the difficulties of tackling the problems of the most excluded. This includes those groups who may be resistant to becoming 'partners', such as young people or Travellers.

Some local partnership projects have made a major contribution by bringing substantial housing, industrial and commercial investment, including private investment, into deprived areas hitherto starved of resources. There is less convincing evidence so far that the most excluded groups, such as the long-term unemployed, have benefited much from new job opportunities. Many relevant factors determining the extent of poverty and exclusion, from the level of social benefits to local employers' policies, lie outside the domain of local partnership.

Consequently, those involved in local partnerships are often sensibly realistic when evaluating their impact on social exclusion, but this can lead to a more fatalistic acceptance that only limited advances can be made. This research suggests that local partnerships need to give continued attention to ensuring that problems of poverty and exclusion are given high priority on their agendas, and that they continually put effort into creating more effective ways to involve and empower the excluded.

The research has focused on areas where there are active and (relatively) well-resourced local partnership projects. The national review of the development of local partnership in the UK pointed, however, to the intensification of problems of poverty and exclusion in recent years, and the widespread nature of such problems. The selective nature of the current resourcing of local partnership initiatives means that the impact of the local partnership approach is partial rather than universal.

Recommendations

- Local regeneration partnerships must ensure that measures to combat poverty and exclusion are high on their agendas and action plans.

- Local partnerships may need to devote more time to advocacy and lobbying external actors and policy makers whose decisions have a major impact on poverty and exclusion within their areas.

Implications and recommendations for partners and stakeholders

The national overview of the local partnership approach to tackling poverty and social exclusion in Chapter 1 reviewed the main categories of partner involvement in the UK, their interests and potential contributions to local partnerships, and their views on the partnership approach. Chapter 2 then gave examples of a number of local partnerships. The case studies that followed in Chapters 3 to 5 showed in more detail how local partnerships draw on the contributions of different partners. This section summarises the main implications for local partners themselves, and for government and EU policies and programmes.

Local government

In many instances, local authorities are the lead or among the leading players in local economic and social regeneration partnerships, and they often have a stronger concern with problems of poverty and social exclusion than some other agencies or private sector partners. Their contribution, and the extent to which partnership strengthens their contribution to local efforts to combat poverty and exclusion, is a vital area to examine.

Local partnerships, such as North Tyneside City Challenge, show that in some cases the local authority can play a very effective leading role in the partnership, including providing managerial and technical support. It is relevant to note that in this case the local authority had promoted a major restructuring of its own organisation to allow it to respond effectively to the demands of partnership. This had involved strengthening its corporate leadership and its research capacity. At the same time, it had retained its own clear agenda alongside its participation in the local partnership. The recent development of partnership in Coventry and Warwickshire shows the value for local authorities of collaborating in local partnerships where solutions to problems involve a city-region or subregional dimension. In the Western Isles and Skye and Lochalsh, partnership promoted collaboration between local authorities with much in common. The LEADER partnership also shows that local authorities can still play an important role where other agencies are taking the lead.

The development in the UK of stronger collaboration between local authorities in tackling poverty and exclusion should enable local government to continue to play a strong role in local regeneration partnerships. It should also help to ensure that issues of poverty and exclusion are given priority. A stronger corporate approach to poverty and exclusion, now being pursued by more local authorities (Alcock et al, 1995), may also be able to involve more fully some departments – education, for example – which are increasingly seen to have a vital role to play in combating exclusion but are often not strongly involved in local partnerships. It may also prompt local authorities to consider their roles as important local employers in the context of local anti-poverty strategies.

A central issue for local authorities is to ensure that there is a positive relationship between the direct representation of local communities in partnerships, and the democratic basis of local government. Some local authority partners appear to tolerate local community representation, rather than seeking ways in which representative local politics and the direct involvement of communities and excluded groups can enhance each other. Local authorities need to recognise that the involvement of excluded groups may at times be uncomfortable for local government, and that cultural change and a review of decision-making processes may still be required if 'empowerment' is to become a reality.

Recommendations

Local authorities:

- often need to reassess existing structures and working practices to facilitate partnership working;

- should consider collaborating with neighbouring authorities as well as private, voluntary and community partners to base partnership on an area where solutions can work;

- should develop stronger corporate approaches to poverty and exclusion;

- should seek to ensure that issues of poverty and exclusion are high on local regeneration partnership agendas;

- should promote positive relationships between democratic local government and community involvement in partnerships.

Other state and quasi-state agencies

Other locally based state and quasi-state agencies play strong roles in local partnerships. In particular, the TECs/LECs are enthusiastic participants because their structure and activity is predicated on local public–private partnership, and they bring to partnerships private sector individuals with an interest in the wider community. The Western Isles and Skye and Lochalsh LEADER partnership shows that TECs/LECs can take a lead role in local partnerships, and can welcome the opportunity that partnerships concerned with poverty and exclusion offer to assist groups who are excluded from, or marginalised in, the local labour market.

Other agencies, such as health and police authorities, can also play very important roles in ensuring that local partnerships take on board community safety and health issues within a multidimensional approach. However, participation in local partnerships concerned with poverty and exclusion challenges quasi-state agencies to adopt broader perspectives than those embodied in their specific functions and remits.

Recommendations

- Like local authorities, other state agencies may need to assess and review their own priorities and procedures to give greater priority to issues of poverty and exclusion, and to maximise their contribution to partnership working.

Employers and employer organisations

The involvement of business in local regeneration partnerships has been strongly promoted by government in the UK. The partnerships in North Tyneside and Coventry and Warwickshire are examples of the important position that private firms and business organisations can have on local partnership structures. Business involvement is both symbolic (for example, the chairmanship of Coventry and Warwickshire Partnerships Ltd by Jaguar) and a means of ensuring that local partnerships reflect local business perspectives and agendas. However, some commentators in the UK suggest that the contribution of business to local partnership is inhibited by the weakness of some Chambers of Commerce, and the close and/or overlapping responsibilities of TECs/LECs, Chambers, and the new Business Links. Individual private sector representatives on partnership bodies are often highly committed, but this does not necessarily produce a wider commitment among the business community, partly because there are often only limited mechanisms in a partnership the individuals and individual businesses involved to consult with and report to other employers in the local economy.

Business involvement is particularly related to aspects of multidimensional local strategies in which the private sector has direct involvement and interest – industrial, town centre and housing developments, for example. Business support may be less evident in relation to the social dimensions of regeneration, including problems of poverty and exclusion. In Coventry and Warwickshire, for example, some business partners would like to see the local partnership confine itself to 'economic' regeneration. Nor do business partners usually play major roles in resourcing and managing local partnerships, and their role as local employers is usually distinct from their partnership role. (This is also the case for public sector employers.)

Recommendations

- Business involvement in local partnerships concerned with poverty and exclusion still often needs to be deepened, including securing the commitment of business to broader strategic objectives as well as to more direct interests.
- One way to achieve more direct involvement by businesses would be if more employers, especially leading firms in local areas, were to become committed to the principles of the European Declaration of Businesses against Social Exclusion (Griffiths, 1995), and to the

practical actions that the Declaration suggests firms as employers should take.

- National bodies representing business, such as the Confederation of British Industry and Business in the Community, should develop and promote clearer guidelines about how employer involvement in local partnerships should be organised.

- In the absence of national initiative in this area, it is important that at the local level there is agreement among private sector partners as to how to promote the effective representation of local business.

Trade unions

Trade unions have an extremely important potential role in local partnerships concerned with poverty and exclusion, because of their direct experience of employment issues. Recent statements by the TUC demonstrate the commitment of the national leadership of the trade union movement to combating exclusion. At a local level, trade unions remain strong in many workplaces and often provide support for facilities for unemployed workers, and (as in Tyneside) take the lead in trying to save jobs.

Despite this, trade unions are generally not well represented on local partnership structures and, when they are represented, do not necessarily make effective use of that representation.

Recommendations

- Trade unions should be much more fully represented on local partnerships concerned with poverty and exclusion.

- The trade union movement, including the TUC and individual unions, should give greater priority to involvement in local partnerships, and to developing the distinctive trade union contribution.

- It should be possible to draw on the examples of other EU countries (Nicaise and Henriques, 1995) to enhance the trade union contribution, especially through the European Trades Union Congress.

Voluntary sector

The research confirms that voluntary sector organisations can play a number of important roles in local partnerships. Voluntary organisations bring direct experience of problems of poverty and exclusion, and close contacts with excluded groups.

In the Western Isles and Skye and Lochalsh LEADER project, for example, voluntary organisations made a major input to developing the innovative approach to cultural development which the partnership adopted. As in other areas, voluntary organisations were also often important partners in specific projects within the partnership programme. On the other hand, in some of the partnerships discussed, voluntary sector organisations did not feel that they had equal status with other agencies. In some, they were under-represented on the core decision-making structures. Larger voluntary agencies now have strong and professional national structures from which they feel they are in a position to contribute to local partnership. New funding mechanisms, including the National Lottery and the Millennium Fund, will strengthen their contribution. If the contribution of the voluntary sector is to be more fully utilised, it may require a greater willingness by other partners to accommodate these organisations, as well as a challenge to voluntary agencies themselves to take a step beyond their established roles.

Recommendations

- More effective guidelines and support may be necessary in national and European programmes to promote a stronger voluntary sector position within partnerships.

- At a local level, voluntary sector agencies need to strengthen their contacts with other organisations to achieve more influence within partnerships, and other partners need to recognise the contribution which voluntary agencies can bring.

- Less experienced voluntary organisations should draw on the guidance provided by national support organisations (Clark, 1995).

The community and excluded groups

Community involvement is, in principle, now a central element of the local partnership approach in the UK. 'Getting the community on board' is recognised by agencies (and the private sector) as a precondition for government and European funding for local regeneration to be secured. However, it is not sufficient for community involvement to be driven primarily by funding requirements: it must reflect an appreciation of the positive benefits both for communities themselves and for other partners.

Many local partnerships have developed and utilised innovative structures and processes of community involvement – for example, the community forums and development trusts in North Tyneside, or the local animators in the Western Isles and Skye and Lochalsh LEADER partnership. It is commonplace (although not universal) for community interests to be represented on local partnership management boards. Community development and other organisations offer training and support for community representatives. Public and private sector representatives acknowledge the role of community representatives in promoting locally sensitive strategies and initiatives. Nonetheless, this and other recent research (Fordham, 1995; McArthur, 1995) shows that community involvement, especially in the more deprived communities, is very often fragile, and 'the community' is far from being an equal partner in most local partnerships. This partly reflects the widely documented tendencies for conflict between community representatives, questions over their legitimacy, and their limited experience in partnership working.

Increasing resources and support – including training, funding of community support organisations and advice – are now being made available to support community involvement in local partnerships, by government (PIEDA, 1995), by local authorities, and by national support organisations (Community Development Foundation, 1995a; 1995b). Private sector organisations are also offering support. This research suggests that this is a necessary and welcome trend, but that support for community involvement needs to be both systematic (not just available) and closely targeted.

Recommendations

Recommendations for community involvement arising from this research reflect the findings that many partnerships currently work more effectively between organisations than with the community and excluded groups.

- Community partners need to develop and maintain agreement to a common 'community strategy' within the partnership.

- If community representatives are to succeed in this, there needs to be systematic resourcing, training and capacity-building for community representation in local partnerships.

- Support is necessary not only for community representatives but to improve the understanding of other partners, including senior figures in partnerships, of the perspectives and needs of excluded groups.

- Local partnership strategies may need to give more priority to the needs and perspectives of local communities and excluded groups.

- Local partnerships can make positive use of the different channels through which local communities' interests are represented – directly, through community organisations, by local councillors, through the experience of public and voluntary agencies and trade unions.

- Partnerships need to adopt a long-term approach and strategy for involving communities and excluded groups. They also need to recognise that community involvement will be enhanced as much as anything by the early success of initiatives improving the quality of life of deprived communities and groups, especially perhaps by demonstrating an ability to meet employment needs.

National government

In the UK, successive recent governments, including the current Labour administration, have strongly promoted the local partnership approach to problems of economic and social regeneration. Government has seen the partnership approach as a means of bringing business perspectives and expertise into public policy and ensuring that local strategies have broad support. The more inclusive framework for local partnership which has progressively emerged through City Challenge and the SRB has been widely welcomed by many public, private and community interests.

However, the local partnership approach has been introduced within a framework of competitive bidding for resources, enabling government to gain greater control over local expenditure. Considerable reservations have been expressed about this element of policy. This includes concerns that local proposals are tailored to match government priorities rather than really reflecting local interests and needs; about the cost in both money and disillusionment of partnership effort put into unsuccessful bids; about the distribution of resources in relation to areas of need. This research has looked primarily at areas where partnership has been sustained by substantial resources, and not at the considerably greater number of areas where this is not the case.

Some of these concerns are apparent, however, even within 'well-resourced' areas. On Tyneside, the success of the City Challenge has highlighted the disparity between areas where investment has been concentrated both within and outside the City Challenge area, and others where such investment is lacking.

A further concern is that the local partnership approach devolves a major degree of responsibility for economic and social regeneration to local agencies and communities, while many important decisions remain exclusively within the control of government itself. City Challenge partners on Tyneside expressed the view that the government's reduction of benefit levels, and other cuts in public spending, outweighed any impact which the local partnership might have on poverty. Many stakeholders in local partnerships might welcome more positive partnership between government and local interests to develop a more proactive national strategy for marginalised areas.

Government has expanded the role of Regional Government Offices in managing the process of bidding for partnership resources. The partners in the two English case-study partnerships welcomed this enhanced regional framework of decision making, especially in promoting greater collaboration between government departments. However, there is still seen to be a need to improve the capacity of the Regional Offices (for example, some business partners questioned the ability of regional officials to assess competitive bids) and to make them more locally responsive.

Recommendations

This research has implications for government policies and programmes in respect of the level and allocation of resources, the relations between government and local partnerships, and the relationship between local policy initiatives and other government policies. If local partnerships are to fulfil their potential in combating poverty and exclusion, government should:

- allocate more resources to programmes funding local partnerships tackling poverty and exclusion; this would draw in more matching funding;

- relate resource allocation more closely to need (while retaining flexibility and encouraging local initiative) both in the distribution of resources between different areas and by giving more priority to issues of poverty and exclusion in guidance for local regeneration bids;

- recognise in programmes and funding regimes the long-term enterprise of building local partnership, especially by continuing to offer systematic support for community participation, and focusing this support on the most disadvantaged groups;

- encourage a stronger partnership approach between government itself, including the Regional Offices, and local partnerships;

- develop a more strategic national policy framework towards problems of exclusion and marginalised areas, within which the contribution of local partnerships can be coordinated with national social and economic policies.

European Union programmes and initiatives

In the UK, national government programmes have been the major force promoting a local partnership approach. However, European programmes have also been significant. In the absence of UK government programmes aimed specifically at combating poverty and exclusion, the successive European Poverty Programmes, and especially Poverty 3, have played an important role. Among many policy makers, especially at local level, there was strong support for a new European programme to follow Poverty 3, but also recognition that more would be needed from a new programme than a limited number of further local experimental projects.

In rural areas, the LEADER programme has been of particular importance in promoting innovative and bottom-up approaches to development through local partnership, as is suggested by the discussion of the Western Isles and Skye and Lochalsh project. In both Scotland and Wales, the perceived strengths of LEADER have influenced recent thinking on the use of the European Structural Funds.

The experience of local partners in both Poverty 3 and LEADER projects suggests, however, that the local impact of future EU programmes would benefit from greater programme flexibility, especially over expenditure conditions, and from more effective exchange of experience between projects and between member states, including more emphasis on evaluation and diffusion of successful projects. The model for future programme organisation should be less top-down, allowing more opportunity for transnational exchange between local partnership projects.

Recommendations

- The European Commission's current review of the Structural Funds and Community Initiatives should prioritise the targeting of resources to areas and social groups experiencing unemployment, poverty and social exclusion.

- Partners and stakeholders in local partnerships in the UK also recognise the benefits of transnational exchange of experience. Future EU programmes should offer greater scope for in-depth exchange of experience and dissemination of achievements between EU countries.

- Lessons from local partnerships tackling poverty and exclusion and from the LEADER projects should be drawn on when developing and implementing Structural Fund programmes and projects, and new initiatives.

Contribution of local partnerships

This research has demonstrated the considerable role that local partnerships can play in combating poverty and social exclusion at the local level. It also suggests that there is a degree of consensus among policy makers both about the gains which can be achieved from effective partnership working, and about some of its costs and current limitations.

The gains from a partnership approach are essentially two-fold.

- Local partnerships can provide a framework which encourages the coordination and integration of policies and resources between the public, private and not-for-profit sectors and with the involvement of excluded communities and groups themselves.

- This can enable social and economic policies to respond more effectively to the local concentrations of poverty and exclusion which are now far more widespread, and introduce a greater degree of differentiation and responsiveness to the needs of excluded communities and social groups.

However, the research also demonstrates that local partnerships are not always able to achieve these gains. In particular, most have achieved only moderate success in involving, and sharing power, with excluded communities. Local partnerships lack the power and resources to deal fully with some of the fundamental problems of poor areas, such as unemployment. In some situations it may be very difficult to develop effective collaboration between key players, and so a partnership approach may not always be the best way to achieve results. Local partnership is only one part of the answer to the major structural problems of poverty and exclusion which now confront the UK, along with other member states of the EU. The research makes it clear that there is no one model of local partnership which can be advanced as the optimum for all contexts. There is a need for continuing flexibility, innovation and experimentation, supported by research and evaluation, to advance good practice.

There is also a justifiable concern that the promotion of local partnership should not become a 'cover' for the fragmentation of policy responses, and lead to a loss of democratic accountability and a reduction in the resourcing of mainstream social programmes. The future of partnership should be within the context of a continuing commitment to a strong public welfare system, and to redistributive fiscal, economic and social policies. It is within such a framework that local partnerships can make the most valuable contribution to dealing with localised problems of poverty and exclusion.

References

Alcock, P., Craig, G., Dalgleish, K. and Pearson, S. (1995) *Combatting local poverty: the management of anti-poverty strategies by local government*, Luton: LGMB.

Amin, K. with Oppenheim, C. (1992) *Poverty in black and white*, London: Child Poverty Action Group.

Arkleton Trust (Research) Ltd and Department of Land Economy, University of Aberdeen (1994) *WISL LEADER evaluation: final report*, Inverness: Arkleton Trust.

Association of County Councils, Association of District Councils and Association of Metropolitan Authorities (1994) *Urban policy: the challenge and the opportunity*, London: ACC/ADC/AMA.

Association of County Councils, Association of District Councils and Association of Metropolitan Authorities (1995) *Local needs, local choice, local government*, London: ACC/ADC/AMA.

Bailey, N. with Barker, A. and Macdonald, K. (1995) 'Brownlow Community Trust', Chapter 5 in *Partnership agencies in British urban policy*, London: UCL Press.

Ball, C. (1994) *Bridging the gulf: improving social cohesion in Europe – the work of the European Foundation for the Improvement of Living and Working Conditions*, EF/94/04/EN, Luxembourg: Office for Official Publications of the European Communities.

Bennett, R.J. and Krebs, G. (1994) 'Local economic development partnerships: an analysis of policy networks in EC-LEDA local employment development strategies', *Regional Studies,* vol 28, no 2, pp 119-40.

Black, S. and Conway, E. (1995) 'Community led rural development in the Highlands and Islands: the European Community's LEADER programme', *Local Economy*, vol 10, no 3, pp 229-45.

Business in the Community (1994) *Regenerating Britain: common purpose, uncommon energy,* London: BIC.

Campbell, B. (1992) *Goliath: Britain's dangerous places*, London: Methuen.

Chanan, G. (1992) *Out of the shadows: local community action and the European Community*, Dublin: European Foundation for the Improvement of Living and Working Conditions.

Chelliah, R. (1995) *Race and regeneration: a consultation document*, London: Local Government Information Unit.

Chester-Kadwell, B., Geddes, M. and Martin, S. (1995) *Local regeneration: a guidance document*, Luton: LGMB.

Clark, G. (1995) *The Single Regeneration handbook: guide to making bids to the Challenge Fund*, London: NCVO.

Coe, T. (1995) *Giving something back: a survey of managers' involvement in the local community*, Luton: Institute of Management/LGMB.

Commission on Social Justice (1994) *Social justice: strategies for national renewal*, London: Vintage.

Community Development Foundation (1995a) *Regeneration and the community: guidelines to the community involvement aspect of the SRB Challenge Fund*, London: CDF.

Community Development Foundation (1995b) *Regeneration and the community: involving the community in the SRB*, London: CDF.

Coopers and Lybrand/Business in the Community (undated) *Growing business in the UK: lessons from Europe: promoting partnership for local economic development and business support in the UK*, London: Coopers and Lybrand.

Coventry and Warwickshire Partnerships Ltd (1994) *Single Regeneration Budget: bid for funding 1995/6 – 1999/2000*, Coventry: CWP Ltd.

Coventry and Warwickshire Partnerships Ltd (1995) *The economic strategy for Coventry and Warwickshire*, Coventry: CWP Ltd.

Coventry City Council (1994) *Hillfields 2000 URBAN Community Initiative*, Coventry: Coventry City Council.

Dahrendorf, R. (ed) (1995) *Report on wealth creation and social cohesion in a free society*, London: Commission on Wealth Creation and Social Cohesion.

Darke, R. (1995) 'Multi-agency partnerships and urban regeneration', Paper to BSA Conference, 'Contested Cities', Leicester: Mimeo.

Davoudi, S. and Cameron, S. (1994) *North Tyneside City Challenge monitoring and evaluation: a baseline report*, Newcastle:

Department of Town and Country Planning, University of Newcastle.

Employment Department Group (1995) *Who cares wins: an employers guide to involvement in the community*, London: EDG.

English Partnerships (1995) *Community investment guide*, London: English Partnerships.

Erskine, A. and Breitenbach, E. (1994) 'The Pilton Partnership: bringing together the social and the economic to combat poverty', *Local Economy*, vol 9, no 2.

Eurostat (1997) *Statistics in focus: income distribution and poverty in EU 12-1993*, Luxembourg: Office for Official Publications of the European Community.

Fordham, G. (1995) *Made to last: creating sustainable neighbourhood and estate regeneration*, York: Joseph Rowntree Foundation.

Gaffikin, F. and Morrissey, M. (1994a) 'Poverty in the 1980s: a comparison of the United States and the United Kingdom', *Policy and Politics*, vol 22, no 1, pp 43-58.

Gaffikin, F. and Morrissey, M. (1994b) 'In pursuit of the Holy Grail? Combating local poverty in an unequal society', *Local Economy*, vol 9, no 2, pp 100-16.

Gaffikin, F. and Morrissey, M. (1995) *The Brownlow Poverty Project evaluation report*, Brownlow: BCT.

Geddes, M. (1995) *The role of partnerships in promoting social cohesion*, Dublin: European Foundation for the Improvement of Living and Working Conditions, Working Paper 38/95/EN.

Green, A.E. (1994) *The geography of poverty and wealth*, Warwick: University of Warwick: Institute for Employment Research.

Griffiths, J. (1995) *Business and social exclusion: a guide to good practice*, London: British Telecom/London Enterprise Agency.

Harding, A. and Garside, P. (1994) 'Urban and economic development', in J. Stewart and G. Stoker (eds), *The future of local government*, London: Macmillan.

Hayden, C. (1994) 'Partnership – sop or solution? Trying to tackle poverty through partnership in Wood End', *Local Economy*, vol 9, no 2, pp 153-65.

House of Lords Select Committee on the European Communities (1994) *The Poverty Programme, evidence of Granby-Toxteth Community Project*, Session 1993-4, 9th Report, London: HMSO.

Industrial Society, The (1995) *Unlocking people's potential,* London: Industrial Society.

Jessop, B. (1994) The transition to Post-Fordism and the Schumpeterian workfare state', in R. Burrows and B. Loader (eds) *Towards a Post-Fordist welfare state?,* London: Routledge.

Joseph Rowntree Foundation (1995) *Inquiry into income and wealth,* York: Joseph Rowntree Foundation.

Kitchin, H., Chelliah, R. and Evans, J. (1994) *Women and urban regeneration,* London: Local Government Information Unit.

Levitas, R. (1996) 'The concept of social exclusion and the new Durkheimian hegemony', *Critical Social Policy,* vol 16, no 1, pp 5-20.

Local Government Management Board (1995) *Partnership in action: case studies of collaboration between TECs and local authorities,* Luton: LGMB.

Local Government Management Board/Environment Trust (1995) *Creating involvement,* Luton: LGMB.

Macfarlane, R. (1993) *Community involvement in City Challenge: a policy report and a good practice guide,* London: NCVO.

Mackintosh, M. (1992) 'Partnership: issues of policy and negotiation', *Local Economy,* vol 7, no 3 ,pp 210-24.

Mawson, J. et al (1995) *The Single Regeneration Budget: the stocktake,* Birmingham: CURS, University of Birmingham.

McArthur, A. (1995) The active involvement of local residents in strategic community partnerships', *Policy and Politics,* vol 23, no 1, pp 61-71.

McLaughlin, B. (1994) 'Studying rural poverty', *Rural Viewpoint,* Autumn, Cirencester: Action for Communities in Rural England.

Meadowell Development Trust (undated) *Meadowell, a peaceful and prosperous community,* North Tyneside: MDT.

Midmore, P., Ray, C. and Tregear, A. (1995) *The South Pembrokeshire LEADER project, an evaluation,* University of Wales: Aberystwyth.

Monks, J. (1995) *Speech to ETUC meeting on social exclusion,* Liverpool, May, London: TUC.

Moore, R. (1997) 'Poverty and partnership in the Third European Poverty Programme: the Liverpool case', in N. Jewson and S. MacGregor (eds) *Transforming cities: contested governance and new spatial divisions,* London: Routledge.

National Council for Voluntary Organisations and Local Government Management Board (1993) *Building effective local partnerships*, London: NCVO.

National Council for Voluntary Organisations (1995) *The Single Regeneration Budget handbook,* London: NCVO.

Nicaise, I. and Henriques, J-M. (1995) *Proceedings of the European Seminar, Trade unions, unemployment and social exclusion,* Leuven: Hooger Instituut voor de Arbeid.

North Tyneside City Challenge Partnership Ltd (1993) Action plan, North Tyneside: NTCCP Ltd.

North Tyneside City Challenge Partnership Ltd (1994) *Action plan,* North Tyneside: NTCCP Ltd.

O'Toole, M., Snape, D. and Stewart, M. (1995) 'Interim evaluation of the Castlemilk Partnership', *Research Findings*, No 12, Scottish Office Central Research Unit, Environment Research Programme, Edinburgh: Scottish Office.

OECD, Territorial Development Service, Group on Urban Affairs (1995) *Urban governance in OECD countries*, Background Paper, Paris: OECD.

Oppenheim, C. (1993) *Poverty: the facts*, London: Child Poverty Action Group.

Peck, J.A. and Tickell, A. (1994) 'Too many partnerships ... the future for regeneration partnerships', *Local Economy*, vol 9, no 3, pp 251-65.

Peck, J.A. and Tickell, A. (1995) 'Business goes local: dissecting the "business agenda" in Manchester', *International Journal of Urban and Regional Research*, vol 19, no 1, pp 55-78.

PIEDA (1994) *North Tyneside City Challenge Ltd: audit of appraisal, monitoring, financial control systems and tendering procedures,* Reading: PIEDA.

PIEDA (1995) *Involving communities in urban and rural regeneration: A guide for practitioners*, London: Department of the Environment.

Rennie, F.W. (1994) *The LEADER programme: a case study*, Edinburgh: Scottish Natural Heritage.

Roberts, V., Russell, H., Harding, A. and Parkinson, M. (1995) *Public/private/voluntary partnerships in local government*, Luton: LGMB.

Robson, B.T. (1994) 'Urban policy at the cross-roads', *Local Economy*, vol 9, no 3, pp 216-23.

Room, G. (1995) *Beyond the threshold: the measurement and analysis of social exclusion*, Bristol: The Policy Press.

Rotherham Metropolitan Borough Council (1995) *Social Policy Bulletin 2, Autumn*, Rotherham: Rotherham MBC.

SPARC (1996) *Chairman's report*, Pembrokeshire: SPARC.

Stewart, M. and Taylor, M. (1995) *Empowerment and estate regeneration*, Bristol: The Policy Press.

Stewart, M. (1994) 'Between Whitehall and Town Hall: the realignment of urban regeneration policy in England', *Policy and Politics*, vol 22, no 2, pp 133-45.

Trades Union Congress (1994) *A new partnership for company training: consultative paper*, London: TUC.

Western Isles and Skye and Lochalsh LEADER (1991) *Submission to the European Community*, Stornoway: WISL LEADER Group.

Western Isles and Skye and Lochalsh LEADER Group (1995) *LEADER II Proposal*, Stornoway: WISL LEADER Group.

Wilcox, D. (1994) *The guide to effective participation*, York: Partnership/Joseph Rowntree Foundation.